CAMRA's

So you want to be a

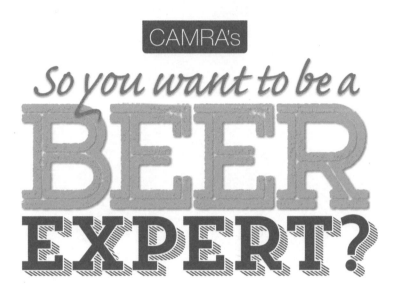

BEER

EXPERT?

BOOKS

Published by the Campaign for Real Ale Ltd.

230 Hatfield Road
St Albans
Hertfordshire AL1 4LW
www.camra.org.uk/books

Design and layout © Campaign for Real Ale Ltd. 2015
Text © Jeff Evans

ISBN 978-1-85249-322-6

A CIP catalogue record for this book is available from the British Library
Printed and bound in Slovenia by GPS Group Ltd.

Head of Publishing: Simon Hall
Project Editors: Katie Button, Julie Hudson
Copy Editor: Simon Tuite
Design/Typography: Hannah Moore
Editorial Assistance: Susannah Lord
Indexer: Cathy Heath
Sales & Marketing: David Birkett

Picture credits: p15 PRISMA ARCHIVO/Alamy Stock Photo; p16 age fotostock/Alamy Stock Photo; p32 Beergenie; p41 Cath Harries; p48 Kent Life; p54 Jeff Evans; p63 Cath Harries, p98 Cath Harries; p123 Chronicle/Alamy Stock Photo; p130 www.milo-profi.be; p165 Jeff Evans; p172 Jeff Evans

CAMRA's

So you want to be a

BEER

EXPERT?

A hands-on guide for the inquiring beer drinker

JEFF EVANS

CAMPAIGN
FOR
REAL ALE

Contents

5: The next step

How the book works

In *So You Want to Be a Beer Expert?*, leading beer writer Jeff Evans draws on many years' experience of hosting beer talks and tastings to present a hands-on course in beer appreciation.

First comes the general introduction to the subject. This may be sufficient for beginners, and it also serves as a quick memory-jogger for those who already have some knowledge. Step two involves a heading called Technicalities which goes into each topic in further detail. Novices may wish to skip over these parts until they feel more comfortable with the subject, but experienced beer fans will gain new knowledge from the sometimes quite complex information presented in this section. For step three, the book hands the initiative back to you.

TASTE OFF!

Each chapter offers one or more Taste off beer selections to try. By comparing the suggested beers, you can discover for yourself how a particular ingredient, technique or beer style affects the beer in your glass, and form your own conclusions

Take the initiative

Coloured boxes throughout the book provide additional information and suggest ways in which you can increase your understanding of beer

Insight

Tip

Insights and Tips give supplementary information about the subject discussed

To become a real subject expert, you need to take things further. Hands on, Visit and Read on boxes point you in the direction of further enlightenment, suggesting activities to try, museums, brewing centres and beer destinations to visit, and additional books to read

1: From the beginning

Introduction

It's a jungle out there. Not so long ago, you could visit your local pub safe in the knowledge that the only beer you were likely to be offered would be bitter, lager or keg stout. Those of us who wanted more didn't like that, of course, but at least it made choosing fairly simple.

It's wonderful to now have such a choice but it can all be a bit bamboozling

Today, that same pub is likely to be serving a far greater selection of beers. Many of these will be variants of bitters, lagers and stouts but, increasingly, even little back-street boozers are expanding their selections to include beers barely heard of just 10 years ago. If you venture into cities, the choice is even more spectacular, with speciality beer bars popping up all over the place. In these, often rather minimalist, venues, the beer range has been maximized. On top of perhaps a dozen or more cask ales, and a similar number of keg beers, you may be tempted by coolers full of bottles, almost as many as you will find in the expanding speciality beer shop sector. The beers come from breweries big and small, from the UK and from other countries. They range in strength from below 3% ABV (alcohol by volume) to well above 10% ABV; they are packed with speciality malts

and flamboyant exotic hops; they come in colours as contrasting as the palest straw, the deepest crimson and the most impenetrable black. A beer world that was once doggedly monochrome has exploded into a rainbow of colours. It's wonderful to now have such a choice but it can all be a bit bamboozling. There seems to be so much knowledge needed today when it comes to selecting the right beer. Try-before-you-buy schemes and the well-informed bar staff undoubtedly help you find your way around the busy bar counter, but there's nothing like having confidence in your own ability. That's where this book comes in and its inspiration comes from a rival business.

The value of education

For decades, the wine trade has been built on education. Those who market wine realized early on that the key to success was to place power in the hands of the consumers. They didn't talk down to them; they didn't take them for granted. Instead, they shared their knowledge. They put information about grapes and techniques and provenance and culture on their bottle labels; they described perfect food pairings; they went out and talked to the customers, offering tasting sessions and explaining all about the product. Customers responded positively. Wine came to be seen as a sophisticated product, something to learn more about. Over time, wine drinkers began to feel that they not only understood the product but also were rather knowledgeable about it. Ringing cash registers testified to a winning formula.

Only in recent years has the beer industry cottoned on to the value of education. Trapped for decades in a race-to-the-bottom cycle of self-deprecation, its business model, on the whole, was based on a combination of patronizing, whimsical adverts and rock-bottom prices. No mention was made of how beers were produced beyond the anodyne 'brewed from the finest ingredients'. Brewers, when questioned about their malts and hops, would often decline to answer, citing commercial confidentiality. Finally, the penny dropped. At last, bottle labels began to have something to say. Even the subject of food-pairing raised its head. The industry began to grow up and to treat its customers like adults. That we live in such an exciting age for beer must, surely, be partly as a result of this change of emphasis.

We now need to take things further, to build on what's been achieved and to foster a demanding beer-drinking public that takes pride in its favourite tipple and will push it to ever-greater heights.

About the book

In a small way, this book is designed to be part of that progress. It is divided into several sections, each dealing with an important facet of beer appreciation. I begin, right at the start of beer's story, by tracing the origins of the drink from a simple grain-based alcoholic beverage in the Middle East to the cosmopolitan industry that spans the world today. I discuss how beer is brewed. Most beer books have a section covering the basics of production but here I go a step further, with a detailed analysis of every stage of the process. It's a level of information that normally is only found on brewing courses, but I hope in this format it is easily accessible to all.

I then talk about the taste of beer, how to appreciate it and how to work out where all those wonderful colours, aromas and flavours come from, as well as how to identify those less welcome flavours that unfortunately crop up from time to time. Next, I branch out into beer styles, exploring the full panoply, revealing their history, how they are made and what to expect in the glass. I also take a good look at procuring beer, with tips on buying, storing and serving, and then I explore the concept of beer judging, where you can formalize your interest and take your involvement in the beer world beyond the simple pleasures of drinking. Finally, there's a section on beer and food, opening the door to a world of culinary possibilities. If you take great pleasure in just drinking beer, imagine how much more there is to be gained when you factor in food.

All of these sections are written to cater for all levels of prior knowledge. If you've only just tasted your first wheat beer or IPA, don't be daunted. The following pages will lead you gently further into the pleasures of beer appreciation. If you're an old hand then you too will, I hope, find plenty of interest and value. To facilitate this, the book takes a three-step approach, with the text divided into clear sections.

First up is the general introduction to the subject, be it malt production, how yeast works or the complexities of Trappist and abbey beers, to mention just three areas. This may be enough for beginners for the moment and it should also serve as a quick memory-jogger for those who already have some knowledge. Step two involves a heading called Technicalities. Here I get stuck into some detail. Novices may wish to skip over these parts until they feel more comfortable with the subject, but experienced beer fans will, I hope, gain new knowledge from the sometimes quite complex information presented in this section. For step three, the book hands the initiative back to you. To become a real expert, you need to take things further; that's why you will find sections with headings such as Hands on, Taste off!, Visit and Read on that point you in the direction of further enlightenment. Readers are given simple experiments to conduct at home, beers to sample alongside each other, places to explore for a deeper understanding, and books and other sources of information to check out to really delve into the heart of the matter. If that all sounds a bit like homework, so be it, but I guarantee it'll be a lot more enjoyable than any you did at school! Think of this book as a primer and use it to lead you to a greater understanding of beer and its heritage.

The idea for this book emerged from the many talks and tutored tastings I host in the UK and in other countries. It is a huge pleasure to welcome people into one of the great passions of my life, to help them get more out of something they already enjoy but perhaps don't truly understand. Even experienced beer drinkers are surprised by what beer has to offer once they scratch beneath the surface. If I had a pint for every person who has told me at the end of a talk that they 'never knew that before', I'd be a very drunk man! I'm hoping this book will elicit the same response.

Jeff Evans

The story of beer

The story of beer begins around 10,000 years ago. We have to say 'around' as there is clearly no exact known moment when beer was invented, or perhaps discovered. We do know, however, where beer is likely to have embarked on its wonderful journey.

From archaeological finds, it is believed that the region called Sumer, between the Tigris and Euphrates rivers in what is modern-day southern Iraq, is where it all began. Ten millennia ago, this was a lush and fertile land. Early peoples living there would have had the benefit of plentiful grain crops that could be used for food. Initially, these crops grew wild and had to be sought out; later the people learnt to cultivate them, taking the seeds and planting them. This led to an end to a nomadic life. Instead of wandering in search of food, people settled in one place and grew the food around them.

From the crops – sometimes types of wheat, sometimes barley, it seems – they learned to take the grains and crush them to make bread. Some grains, they discovered, could also be turned into a nutritious drink that lifted their spirits. Beer was born.

Prehistory

There is some speculation as to how beer first came into existence. It has been suggested that it happened spontaneously, with wet and sprouting grains being attacked by wild yeasts. Some brave soul dared to taste the foaming, fizzing liquid and declared it worth repeating. Experiments in recreating this scenario, however, have unravelled this possibility, with the liquid generated being so unappetizing that it is unlikely that anyone would have taken a shine to it.

It seems far more likely that brewing was controlled, to at least some degree, from the start, with people perhaps realizing that grain that had been allowed to shoot had a sweeter taste that was further improved by baking it into cakes or loaves of bread. These loaves, perhaps flavoured with fruit or honey, may then have been mashed down in water to make a drink. As fruit and wild honey both carry yeast, the sugars released by the grains were fermented and the liquid became beer. Perhaps there was some serendipity involved at the outset, with the loaves accidentally getting wet, but it's clear that these early brewers soon knew what they were doing. In fact, it has been suggested by some commentators that beer, rather than food, was the primary aim of the process and that the grain was baked into bread not to eat but in order to start the conversion of starches into fermentable sugars. The bread was then soaked to release the sugars and the spent grains – only then – were used for food. The mists of time, as ever, obscure the truth but a similar concept survives in Russia, where an historic form of beer known as kvass is still made by baking bread to use in the mash.

Large-scale breweries were constructed to supply the Pharaoh's court

Ancient civilizations

By the time of around 4000BC, we are quite sure that brewing was a well-practised art. Shards of pottery from that time, containing the residue of primitive beer, have been found, and a couple of thousand years later a hymn to the Sumerian goddess Ninkasi, discovered on a clay tablet, not only reveals the religious value of the drink to the people of the time but actually describes the brewing process in use, including baking bread and soaking grains. And it wasn't just in old Iraq that this was happening. In those days, an arc of good agricultural land known as the Fertile Crescent stretched across the Middle East and beer became a staple of life in areas such as Assyria and the Nile valley. It became particularly popular in Egypt where, possibly as early as around 3000BC, large-scale breweries were constructed to supply the Pharaoh's court and the many slaves who toiled building pyramids and tombs. We know this from evidence found in those tombs – not just pictures and hieroglyphs but also drinking vessels and straws. The straws were used to access the liquid from beneath the debris of grains and yeast. Clearly the Egyptians and other early imbibers did not believe in efficient filtration.

The production of beer subsequently spread to other parts of the world, as the climate changed and northern countries became more suited to grain cultivation. In Britain, archaeological evidence suggests that Neolithic peoples were brewing by around 4000BC. By the time of the Romans, there was already a demarcation between the grain-cultivating, beer-drinking north of Europe and the grape-growing, wine-drinking south. The conquering Romans – like the wine-obsessed Greeks who preceded them – were initially not impressed but they soon came to see the benefits of a drink made from fermented cereals, certainly in their farmost outposts.

The Middle Ages

After the decline of the Roman Empire, beer remained popular among the various tribes that inhabited northern Europe but Roman input continued via the religion they had spread from Rome. In the numerous abbeys and monasteries that opened up, the brethren brewed their own beer. It provided

In *Germany* brewing was once banned during summer months

safe drinking liquid where water supplies may have been unreliable and allowed monks to show hospitality to pilgrims and other travellers. Great houses also began production, leading to the construction of the largest breweries seen for millennia. In the Middle Ages the first ale houses arrived in Britain, when the best female brewers – for it was generally the women who brewed and baked while the menfolk did the hunting and farming – started selling their excess beer. Beer in those days was not the drink we know today. Hops only began to be widely used around the start of the 11th century, when brewers realized that this strange, wiry plant had a preservative quality that helped keep the beer fresh. They also admired its bitterness, the ideal counterpoint to the sweetness of malted barley. Previously, many brewers had relied on a mixture of herbs to balance the taste of their beer, perhaps bog myrtle or ground ivy. In some parts of Europe, a special mixture of herbs known as gruit was sold to brewers. The ingredients involved were not declared but the concoction was a real moneyspinner for the Church or other authorities that controlled its supply. Understandably, the clergy were not best pleased when hops started to erode their business but their efforts to maintain control of brewing proved fruitless. Hopped beer spread across Europe and brewing became an important industry, regulated by city-states and regions to ensure quality. Cities such as Hamburg and Einbeck gained a mighty reputation for their beer, which was exported across the Baltic Sea and was a core trading commodity in what became known as the Hanseatic League.

All beers were still at this stage variants on the ale style. It took a new law in Bavaria to change things. Declaring the summer months unsuitable for brewing, because the warmer weather allowed more bacterial and wild yeast spoilage of fermenting beer, Duke Albrecht V decreed that brewing should end in spring and only recommence in autumn. Brewers therefore brewed a quantity of beer to tide them over, keeping it fresh by storing it in caves filled with ice cut from frozen lakes. In this way, they developed cold conditioning and unintentionally isolated strains of yeast that worked well in colder conditions. Lager was born.

Hops arrived in British brewing in the early 1400s. They were resisted at first but soon charmed the people. The term 'beer' began to be used in the British Isles to describe the new bitter beer that included hops, leaving the earlier name 'ale' for the sweet, unhopped brews of the past. Gradually, even 'ale' began to incorporate some hops and, by around the turn of the 18th century, the two terms had become increasingly interchangeable.

Beer was also taken to the New World. It is reported that the Mayflower only settled at Plymouth (in today's Massachusetts) because the Pilgrim Fathers had run out of beer on their voyage and needed to brew some more.

Commercial brewing

In Britain, beer moved out of the domestic kitchen and into commercial breweries. Porter became the world's first mass-market beer. Brewers discovered that this dark, rich beer aged very well and so built huge vessels in which to keep it. Economies of scale began to play a part and saw fortunes made by pioneers such as Truman and Whitbread. As the Industrial Revolution took hold, the use of steam for power in the brewhouse dynamically changed the mechanics of beer production while an innovative way of drying malt – so that it remained light in colour – fundamentally altered the nature of the product. New paler beers – initially shipped to outposts of the British Empire in India – sent porter into a steady decline, and the creation of the world's first pale lager in Bohemia paved the way for pilsner's domination of the beer world that continues to this day.

With railway networks now tracking across the Continent, beer crossed boundaries more easily than before. Refrigeration transformed brewhouse practices and made production possible year-round. The heat treatment radically expounded by French scientist Louis Pasteur also helped make beer more widely enjoyed, as unwanted bugs that might turn a beer sour could be killed off before it left the brewery (although many drinkers have been cursing the negative flavour consequences of pasteurization ever since). More scientific refinements cleaned up beer's act. Danish scientist Emil Christian Hansen, working at Carlsberg, isolated the purest lager yeast and made it available to the world, so beer became cleaner than ever.

Throughout all these advances brewers, in many cases, continued to respect local traditions. While lager brewing began in Britain in the 1870s, it remained a predominantly ale country until the end of the 20th century. Belgium, too, while giving up most of its market share to pilsner clones, nevertheless clung to its ale traditions, as well as its seemingly primitive method of spontaneous fermentation, in which beer is fermented by wild yeasts in the environment. The US, meanwhile, became a crucible of brewing styles in the late 19th century as immigrants flooded in from all over the globe. All kinds of beers were produced in America but Prohibition changed that. From 1920 to 1933 the production and sale of beer (and other alcohol) were outlawed in the US. Hundreds of breweries went out of business. When the ban was lifted, those that had survived – by diversifying into small beer, soft drinks, malted milk and the like – decided to keep their finances tight by focusing on pale lager beer, made thin and cheap through the use of ingredients such as rice and maize. It slotted nicely into a world of bland convenience foods where spongy bread came ready sliced and cheese was served processed and prepacked. Still brewery numbers fell. It wasn't until the 1970s, with brewery numbers collapsing to less than a hundred, that American beer began to show genuine diversity again, with pride once more playing a part in beer production. Since that time the country has reinvented its brewing industry and reimagined how beer can be. It has become a powerhouse of brewing, exporting its vibrant ideas back to the rest of the world.

Decline and growth

In Britain, ale continued to dominate sales, despite a fall in strength during the 20th century, caused largely by wartime restrictions on barley and malting. Mild ale remained the country's best-selling beer style until the turn of the 1960s, when bitter took over. But technological changes were about to play a hand. Since the 1930s brewers had been experimenting with a new kind of convenience beer, one that had a long shelf life and was easy to transport and serve. Filtered and pasteurized, the 'dead' beer was packed into metal containers called kegs and given some semblance of life through artificial carbonation. This was all in complete contrast to the way beer had been produced for centuries, where yeast lived and worked in the cask of beer right up to the time it was consumed. With brewery mergers and takeovers stifling choice and enabling brewers to dictate which beers went on sale, keg beer began its march. If keg beers had been full of flavour, brewers might have got away with it, but instead they made these beers not only weaker than traditional beers but also often from inferior ingredients. The British drinking public did not take this lying down. In 1971, CAMRA was founded to fight back against keg beer and the devious practices of the big breweries. Slowly, through the 1970s, traditional cask ale – or real ale as CAMRA called it – made a comeback. New breweries began opening to replace some of those closed by the big companies who themselves were forced to backtrack and reintroduce some traditional beer in their pubs. Through the 1980s and 1990s the real ale revival gathered pace, with new breweries arriving nearly every month. With changes to laws to free pubs from the grip of big breweries and to allow the sale of guest beers, the British brewing scene changed dramatically, only to be kicked into overdrive by new tax reductions for small breweries early in the new millennium.

While cask and keg ale had been fighting it out, however, Britain had turned into a lager nation. Supported by mass advertising, keg lager brands became the country's biggest sellers and, by 1990, lager had overtaken ale – both cask and keg combined – as the nation's most purchased beer, going on to peak at

Read on

Jessica Boak and Ray Bailey, *Brew Britannia* (Aurum, 2014)

Pete Brown, *Man Walks into a Pub* (Macmillan, 2003)

Martyn Cornell, *Beer: The Story of the Pint* (Headline, 2003)

Ian S Hornsey, *A History of Beer and Brewing* (Royal Society of Chemistry, 2003)

Patrick E McGovern, *Uncorking the Past: The Quest for Wine, Beer and Other Alcoholic Beverages* (University of California Press, 2009)

Roger Protz and Adrian Tierney-Jones, *Britain's Beer Revolution* (CAMRA Books, 2014)

TASTE OFF!

Historic beers

Here are three beers that offer a glimpse of what beer might have tasted like in the days before hops became a common ingredient.

Williams Bros Fraoch Heather Ale

This beer does include some First Gold hops but the character of the beer comes from its herb and spice additions, primarily heather flowers, bog myrtle and ginger. Note the peppery flavour and the delicate floral notes, but also the full sweetness of the malt.

Gentse Gruut Amber

One of a series of hop-free beers brewed by this specialist Belgian brewery. Surprisingly, it is not too sweet. There are toffee-like malt notes but also a balancing herbal bitterness. The herbs (exact varieties undeclared) are not too heavy, just giving a softly perfumed flavour.

Williams Bros Alba

Harking back to the Viking influence in Scotland, in incorporating spruce sprigs, pine and bog myrtle, this is a slender beer for the strength, with lots of fruit and floral esters. The pine resin note is gentle in the taste but comes through more strongly in the very dry, bitter finish.

around 75% of the market. Ale is now fighting back. Cask ale, in particular, has seen a strong resurgence, at the expense of keg, although a new breed of keg ales – inspired by beers from the new wave of American breweries, which are full of flavour and not usually pasteurized – has complicated the picture.

Today's beer drinkers are better served than at any time in history. Just 50 years ago, it seemed as if all the colour was going to be drained from our glasses. Breweries were getting bigger, choice was getting smaller and quality was diminishing by the day. Who would have thought that the beer world in the early 21st century would be filled with tens of thousands of small and medium-sized breweries, in countries as diverse as Japan and Brazil, Norway and Australia, turning out beers of all shades and strengths, be they authentic reproductions from brewing's past or innovative creations conjured up in the fertile minds of passionate brewers? We could not have recognized a landscape filled with specialist beer bars, of pubs stocking a vast range of beers, and of independent retailers whose shelves and fridges overflow with beer goodies. We could only have dreamed of the ease of travel that allows us to savour at first hand the brewing heartlands of the world and appreciate the beer culture of other nations.

Ten thousand years after the first brewers took wild grains and turned them into beer, we live in a beer world that is more vibrant and colourful than ever.

Visit

Thanks to a growing public interest in beer tourism, there are now dozens of fine brewery museums and visitor centres around the world offering insights into brewing's past, albeit it, in many cases, through the prism of their own company's heritage. More specifically, for a flavour of beer before the arrival of hops, take a trip to Ghent, Belgium, and call in at the **Gruut Brewery** (www.gruut.be). This modern brewery specializes in gruit beers,

shunning hops in favour of the herbs-and-spices blend once universal in these parts. In the same region, an insight into a later, but pre-industrial, era can be enjoyed at **De Snoek Mout en Brouwhuis Museum** (www.desnoek.be) at Alveringem. Here you can see how beer used to be made in the 19th century.

The most comprehensive UK attraction is at Burton upon Trent,

where the well-equipped **National Brewery Centre** (www.nationalbrewerycentre.co.uk) covers all the basics and then goes on to focus on the specialities of its home town – pale ale and IPA. The working model of the town's inter-brewery railway system during its heyday is always a delight.

2: How beer is brewed

The magic of brewing

What is beer? It sounds an obvious question but how often is it ever asked? People, even seasoned beer lovers, seldom query what is in the glass or, more to the point, what it is doing there. For this reason, whenever I host a beer tasting event, I always start right at the beginning, by talking about beer, what it is, how it is made and what ingredients and processes are involved. If I don't do this, I'm pretty sure that many people in the room are not going to fully understand where the colours, aromas and flavours in their glass are coming from, and that defeats the object of the exercise.

So, it's worth asking again, what is beer? Put simply, beer is an alcoholic beverage made by fermenting sugars extracted from a cereal crop. The crop used may vary around the world, with countries and regions traditionally favouring cereals that have been grown locally. In the Orient, rice may be used; in Africa, sorghum; in South America, maize; around the Baltic, rye; in various parts of Europe, wheat. However, by far the most popular cereal for making beer is barley.

Barley is simply perfect for making beer. It renders good extract that can be used for fermentation and its sweet flavours marry perfectly with the other major flavouring ingredient in beer, namely hops. That said, barley is not a simple product from which to extract brewing sugars. Let's make a basic comparison with the making of wine. If you take grapes and crush them, you will release plenty of sweet, sugary juice that is ripe for fermenting. Just add yeast and fermentation will take place. The yeast will eat up the sugar and convert it into alcohol and carbon dioxide. Within a relatively short period of time, you have a primitive form of wine.

Unfortunately, it's not that simple with barley. It's tempting to think that if you crush a bag of barley grains into a tub of water, the sugars will seep out, the water will become sweet and yeast, if added, can perform the same trick as it does with grape juice. Sadly, that is not the case, because the sugars are trapped inside the barley in the form of starches, and these starches need to be released and converted into sugars before the brewer can begin work.

In order for barley to be usable by a brewer, it has to be turned into what is known as malted barley, or malt. The barley grains are shipped from the farm to a special facility known as a maltings. Here they are moistened to encourage them to begin germinating. The germination process, which takes a few days, unlocks the starches vital to brewing and then the maltster dries the grains in a kiln. Some grains are heated more strongly in order to develop different types of malt, which will darken beers and bring such flavours as caramel, nut, coffee and chocolate.

At the brewery, the brewer selects the desired combination of malts, crushes the grains and combines them with hot water in a vessel generally known as the mash tun or mash mixer. The mash is allowed to stand for about an hour, so that the starches in the grains are released into the water. While mashing takes place, natural enzymes in the grain begin to work on the starches, turning them into sugars that can be fermented by yeast. Eventually, the liquid – now called wort – is run off from the mash tun, leaving behind the spent grains. These are of no further use to the brewer and are taken away for animal feed.

Brewers can create an array of flavours using just malt and hops

The wort is now ready for the next stage of beer making but it is remarkable to reflect that it has taken all this effort – soaking the grains, germinating them, drying and cooking them in a kiln, and then mashing them at the brewery – to arrive at the same point as crushing a bunch of grapes in wine making. But, while the process has been somewhat convoluted, it has also allowed the maltster to furnish brewers with a wonderful array of colours and flavours they can play with when creating beers.

With the wort prepared, in theory yeast could now be added and fermentation would begin, but what you'd end up with would be a very sweet, cloying drink. Even though some of the sugars would be eaten up by the yeast as it ferments the beer, a lot of sugars would remain. So, the wise brewer looks to take the edge off that sweetness.

The wort is transferred to a second vessel called the copper or the kettle, where the wort is boiled. Boiling sterilizes the liquid and also allows other flavourings to be added. These are provided by hops.

Hops belong to the same botanical family as the nettle and cannabis. They grow tall and wiry, producing green, conical flowers that attract the brewer for a number of reasons. Firstly, the oils and resins from these flowers contain a natural preservative that helps ward off infections and keep beer fresh. Secondly, they have a deep bitterness, ideal for balancing out the sweetness of the wort. Thirdly, they also bring other flavours to a beer – anything from grassy and herbal to floral and fruity, depending on the variety of hop used.

The brewer will use the boiling process to extract these important attributes from the hops. Because of the wide variety of hops that is available, and the contrasting flavours and aromas each variety brings, the brewer can at this point dramatically change the flavour of the wort. We've already seen how brewers have an extensive range of malts to play with when devising beer recipes. Now we can see that they have a similar selection of hop flavours to choose from, too, and this is where the artistry of the brewer comes in. By mixing and matching malts and hops, brewers can create some astonishing beers, just as top chefs, with their culinary know-how, can produce an outstanding dish from simple ingredients.

After an hour or so in the copper, the heat is turned off and the wort – now known as hopped wort – is run out, leaving behind spent hops, which are of no further use, except perhaps as compost. The liquid is cooled and transferred into a fermentation vessel where yeast is added and fermentation begins.

Yeast is a single-celled fungus that loves to eat sugar. As it does so, it releases alcohol and carbon dioxide. Over a period of around five days, the yeast tucks into the abundant sugars in the hopped wort, filling the liquid with carbonation and steadily increasing the alcoholic strength. It also multiplies furiously and, at an appropriate point, most is skimmed away. Some yeast remains in what is now a basic form of beer, known as green beer because it needs time to mature. The yeast aids this maturation process by nibbling away at remaining sugars and cleaning up unwelcome chemical compounds that have been created as the beer sits in the fermentation vessel or in a separate tank.

It is in these fermentation and maturation stages that the major division in the world of beer takes place, with ales and lagers going their separate ways. Essentially, ales are fermented at a warmer temperature than lagers. They also generally have a short maturation period, whereas lagers can mature – or condition, to use the technical word – for weeks, if not months. By storing the beer for this length of time at very low temperatures, a crisp, clean, smooth beer can be produced which contrasts with the fuller-bodied, fruitier characteristics of an ale.

The length of time an ale matures varies according to the style and strength of the beer. Barley wines and old ales, for example, may be conditioned in a similar way to lager beers, although often at a higher temperature, but most ales are conditioned for perhaps a week after the first fermentation (primary fermentation) has ended. What happens next to the beer depends on the form of packaging it is destined to be sold in.

How beer is brewed

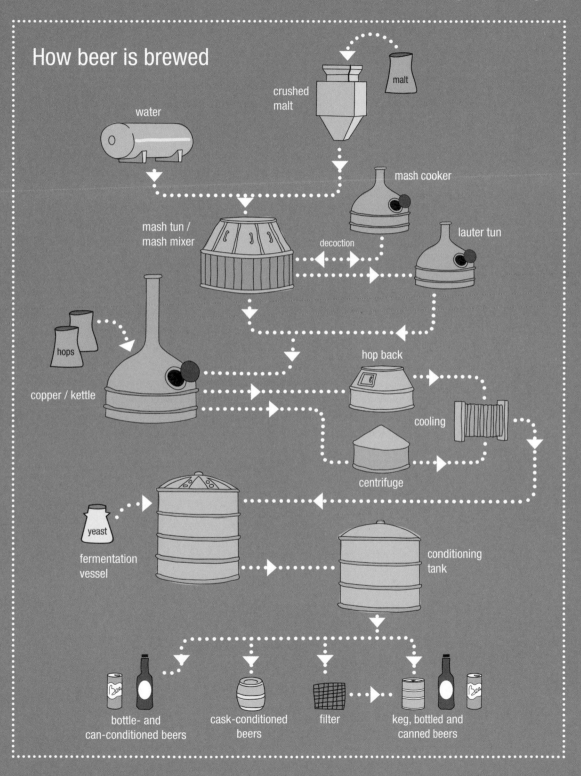

malt

crushed malt

water

mash cooker

mash tun / mash mixer

decoction

lauter tun

hops

hop back

copper / kettle

cooling

centrifuge

yeast

fermentation vessel

conditioning tank

bottle- and can-conditioned beers

cask-conditioned beers

filter

keg, bottled and canned beers

Barley

Barley is a type of grass that has been cultivated as a food crop for millennia. It is a particularly hardy cereal that grows in most parts of the world but generally it prospers best in temperate climates where it is not too hot. Barley was once part of many staple diets, its grains ground into flour and baked into bread. Today, however, most barley is used for animal fodder, or dehusked for cookery under the name pearl barley or, of course, employed for making beer and whisky.

Barley, generally speaking, comes in two types. The first is six-row barley, which, as its name implies, develops six rows of seeds (kernels) at the top of its stalk. The second is the equally appropriately named two-row barley. Six-row is a tougher plant, grown in warmer climates, but brewers mostly prefer the softer, more delicate, better-yielding and less husky nature of two-row. Barley also differs depending on when it is planted. Plants sown in the autumn need to be more durable, to survive the onslaught of winter. These are known as winter barley, and some brewers, particularly ale brewers, appreciate the robust quality that carries through to the beer. The alternative is spring barley, sown after winter has blown away. These plants are more delicate and are favoured by brewers of softer beers, such as delicate golden lagers.

Just like other plants, barley comes in different varieties, some of which work well for brewing and others which do not. Over time, brewers have come to prefer certain varieties, and barley breeders have successfully combined favoured varieties to create new, even more popular, hybrids. In the UK, the barley most popular with brewers is called Maris Otter, but it is not so widely grown today, as big breweries, which use enormous quantities of malt, prefer cheaper alternatives. Those less concerned with counting the pennies appreciate the better extract that Maris Otter brings and its richness of flavour, and therefore are content to pay a small premium to keep the variety in production. That said, other malts can also deliver high-quality beers and each brewer tends to have a firm favourite, often recognizing that this is the variety that the brewery's yeast enjoys working with most, so the choice to not use Maris Otter is not always just a matter of cost.

Visit

Some barley farms now actively encourage the public to understand more about their crop. Look out for their open days when you may get the chance to walk through a barley field, watch the combine harvester at work and learn more about barley's cultivation and uses. One such farm is **Branthill Farm** (www.therealaleshop.co.uk), near Wells-next-the-Sea in Norfolk, England, which has a mini-maltings that visitors can play around in (as well as a bottled beer shop) on site.

Varieties of barley

Some varieties of barley used for brewing in the UK (other parts of the world have their own favoured varieties):

Winter barley	Summer barley
Cassata	Concerto
Flagon	Golden Promise
Maris Otter	Optic
Pearl	Propino
Winsome	Publican
	Quench
	Tipple

Technicalities

Barley (*Hordeum vulgare*) belongs to the *porceae* family of grasses and originated in the Middle East. It has a long stalk of just under a metre (about three feet) tall, with its kernels presented in lines on opposite sides at the top (the ear). Evidence of barley cultivation dates back to around 8000BC and, from archaeological discoveries, we know it has been used for beer making since at least 4000BC. Today, the world's fourth-largest cereal crop, barley grows very well near coastlines, on land that once sat under the sea. Such maritime barley, as it is known, is an important crop in areas such as East Anglia in the UK or Flanders in northern Belgium.

Malting

As outlined earlier, barley has to be processed before it can be turned into beer, as the vital starches, which will become fermentable sugars when brewing begins, need to be unlocked. This takes place at a maltings. Here maltsters soak the grains of barley in water for a few days, to moisten them. The grains are then spread on a floor and, over a period of a further few days, are regularly turned to allow oxygen to reach each one. The moisture of the grains, the oxygen in the environment and the gentle humidity of the floor have a miraculous effect on the grains. The barley is tricked into thinking it is springtime – time to start growing. Little roots start to appear as germination kicks in. At the same time, those important starches that have been trapped inside each grain become accessible. Now the maltsters step in again. Of course, they don't want to grow a room full of barley plants so they must now terminate the germination. To do this, they remove the grains to a kiln and blow hot air over them. The grains quickly dry out and the rootlets are then broken off. The barley – now malted barley – is ready to be taken to the brewery.

However, the maltsters' work is not finished. With the grains being dried in the kiln, another dimension can be added to the malt. Heat can be cranked up, allowing the grains to cook, becoming darker the longer they remain in the oven and the greater the heat that is applied. Maltsters can also adjust the humidity of the kiln, so that malt can stew in a steamy atmosphere. This means that they can not only prepare delicately dried, very pale-coloured malt, but also malts with greater character and deeper colours. In a sense, it is like roasting coffee beans. The malts that are delicately treated in the kiln – pale ale malt (usually just called pale malt) and the even paler pilsner and lager malts – have a very light colouring, perfect for producing blond ales and golden lagers, for example.

Darker malts obviously make beer darker in colour but they also mean richer flavours. Pale malt and lager malt have rather neutral flavours when used on their own. They bring sweetness and perhaps delicate, grainy, biscuity notes. Dark malts offer anything from caramel and nut to coffee and chocolate. But dark malts cannot be used on their own because the intensive heat treatment destroys enzymes inside the grains that are needed to convert the starches into fermentable sugars. Consequently, when brewers want to make a dark beer, they will use mostly pale malt or another base malt such as pilsner malt and just a small percentage of the darker speciality grains. The pale malt, with its abundant starches and viable enzymes, can provide the sweetness and the sugar for fermentation; the darker grains add colour and flavour.

The process just outlined is now heavily mechanized in many maltings. The traditional method of spreading the grains on a floor and turning them by hand (floor malting) is only practised in a handful of places, but many brewers prefer this old-fashioned approach as they believe the malt is treated more gently and delivers better results as a consequence. Modern maltings use linked vessels housed in tall, cylindrical towers, where grains can be steeped, turned, germinated and kilned simply by pressing buttons or allowing a computer to take the lead. These tower maltings are very efficient, with faster germination and kilning times and important economies of scale, if somewhat impersonal.

Technicalities

The malting process, as already explained, begins by soaking the grains in water. This process, known as steeping, takes place in large tanks, after the grain has been cleaned (screened) to get rid of foreign bodies, such as small stones. The water temperature is set at a spring-like 11–15ºC (52–59ºF), thus encouraging the grains to begin to germinate. The water – aerated to provide oxygen, to rouse the grains and to ensure they take up water equally – is refreshed two or three times, with the grain allowed an air rest of up to 12 hours before each refilling so that it can breathe. After two to three days, the moisture content of the grain has risen to around 45% and it can be moved on to the next stage.

For germination, whether this is done on a traditional floor or in a computerized facility, the grains are held at around 15ºC (59ºF) and are raked and turned (either by hand or mechanically) on a regular basis to keep the heat even, to prevent them sticking together and to allow air to circulate between them. The bed of malt on a floor is around 20mm (just under an inch) deep and is known in the trade as a couch.

Over the course of around five days, the germination takes hold and rootlets (known as chits) that began to appear during steeping now show prominently.

Hands on

Pay a visit to a home-brewing shop or arrange a tour of your local microbrewery. These will often allow you to inspect different types of malt. Taste each malt individually, starting with the palest. See what flavours you detect.

In a traditional *floor maltings* the grains are raked by hand

Inside a grain of barley

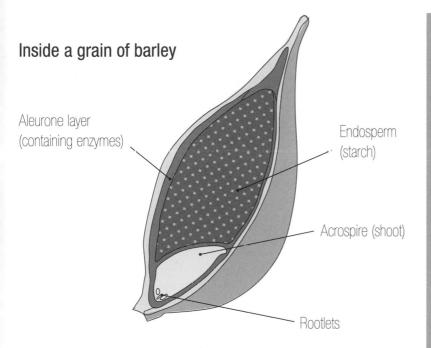

Aleurone layer
(containing enzymes)

Endosperm
(starch)

Acrospire (shoot)

Rootlets

Visit

Some maltings are now open for tours. In most cases, these have to be booked and may be for groups only, such as the tour at **Weyermann** (www.weyermann.de) in Bamberg, Germany. However, **Tucker's Maltings** (edwintucker.co.uk) in Newton Abbot, Devon, has been opened up as a major tourist attraction. Roughly from Easter to the end of October, you can find out all about the malting process with a self-guided tour that leads you from stage to stage with the help of historic artefacts, mannequins and static displays. You can even taste some beer made from the malt produced on site.

At the same time, the shoot of the barley – correctly known as the acrospire – begins to grow inside the grain, between the outer husk and the body of the grain, which is known as the endosperm. The endosperm contains the starches – the plant's natural food supply – which are opened up as a result. Germination is halted when the acrospire has grown inside the grain to about three-quarters the length of the endosperm.

It is not only starches that are released at this stage. A variety of enzymes living within a thin skin called the aleurone layer, which is wrapped around the endosperm, are activated. Their role for the plant – once germination begins – is to break down its natural food supply (the stored starches) into simple nutrition that the plant can use to grow. For the brewer, this enzyme activity is important because it softens up the endosperm, breaks down natural proteins that hold the starches in place into small enough particles that help create good foam and mouthfeel in a beer and, most importantly, converts starches into sugars that can be fermented by the brewer's yeast. This process – known as modification or conversion – begins at the maltings but is completed in the mash tun at the brewery. The most important enzyme group for converting starches are known as amylases.

Read on

John Mallett, *Malt: A Practical Guide from Field to Brewhouse* (Brewers Publications, 2014)

UK Malt: The UK Malting Industry Site (www.ukmalt.com)

After germination, the grains must be dried. Whether in an old-fashioned kiln or a modern tower, it is hot air that dries the grain, which is now known as green malt. To create pale ale malt, one of the lightest-coloured malts, for the first two days the temperature of the air blowing through the grain is maintained at around 65°C (149°F). This gently eliminates most of the moisture, kills off the acrospire and stops the germination, thus preventing the growing plant from using up its starches, which are now wanted by the brewer instead. The enzymes, however, are not damaged. For the final day, the temperature is ramped up to 90°C (194°F) to cure and crisp up the grain. As the grain leaves the kiln, a sieve removes the rootlets which, renamed culms, are often used for animal feed.

Visually, there remains little difference between unmalted barley and pale ale malt, except for a slightly more open and relaxed husk in the malt. However, if you try to bite into a grain of each, the contrast is immediate. The unmalted barley is stone-like (careful with your teeth!) and has little taste, whereas the malt is much softer and quickly releases sweet flavour. The technical term for this softness is friability.

Producing darker malts involves taking a base malt such as pale ale or lager malt and putting it back in the kiln, or a drum roaster. There, the temperature is raised and the grain is literally roasted. Amber malt, slightly darker than pale ale malt, is baked at around 180°C (356°F), to develop a richer biscuit note, while chocolate malt – deep brown in colour – is roasted at around 200°C (392°F) or more and brings flavours of chocolate and coffee.

The creation of some coloured malts involves more complicated uses of heat. Crystal malt – the malt widely used alongside pale ale malt to give that distinctive light-brown colour to British bitters – is created by taking green malt and trapping a high level of humidity from the damp grain in the kiln or drum. With the temperature raised to around 70°C (158°F), the starches inside the grain liquefy during this stewing process and are immediately converted into sugars by the enzymes. The kiln is then ventilated and the temperature is raised to around 140°C (284°F) or higher to cure the grains. This not only darkens them but also causes the newly created sugars to crystallize. The sweet flavours they bring to brewing are of biscuit, caramel, toffee and nut. Crystal malt can come in a variety of colours, from light to dark, depending on the roasting temperature and the time in the kiln.

A further option is smoked malt, in which smoke from fires built of peat or beechwood, for instance, is allowed to waft over the grains, echoing the primitive form of malting that took place before the advances of the Industrial Revolution.

Types of malt

The table below shows the most common types of malt produced for brewing in increasing order of darkness. Their colours are defined according to two scales. One is stipulated by a technical body called the European Brewing Convention; the other is known as degrees Lovibond, after the brewer who devised the scale in the 19th century. Both scales give the lowest figures to the lightest colours.

Malt type	Approx. EBC / Lovibond colour	Common uses
Lager/pilsner malt	2.5/1.5	Golden ales, pale lagers
Wheat malt	3/1.7	Golden ales, weizens
Pale ale malt	4.5/2.2	Pale ales
Vienna malt	5–8/2.4 2.8	Amber lagers, märzens
Mild ale malt	9–15/3.9–6.2	Milds
Munich malt	12–15/5.1–6.2	Dark lagers
Caramalt	35/13.5	Pale ales
Amber malt	65/25	Dark ales
Brown malt	110/42	Porters
Crystal malt	145/55	Amber ales, bitters
Chocolate malt	1060/400	Dark milds, porters, stouts
Roasted barley	1220/460	Porters, stouts
Black malt	1280/480	Porters, stouts

Lager malt   Pale ale malt   Amber malt   Crystal malt

Chocolate malt   Roasted barley   Black malt

Insight 🔍

One good reason for the use of adjuncts is to create a beer that conforms to the definition of gluten-free. Gluten is a protein that sufferers of coeliac disease struggle to break down during digestion. It is found in wheat, barley and rye, which means beers containing these cereals can pose a problem for sufferers. Early gluten free beers made use of alternative cereals to provide fermentable sugars, most commonly sorghum. In recent times, however, some brewers, including Hop Back and Westerham in the UK and Daas in Belgium, have found ways of reducing the gluten content of their barley beers to below the acceptable threshold, thus giving drinkers a more authentic flavour when drinking gluten-free. Guarding their commercial advantage, these brewers are rather secretive about the processes they use to achieve these results, although the use of an enzyme to break down the gluten is increasingly common.

Adjuncts

Malted barley is not the only cereal used to make beer. Other cereals may also be added during the brewing process. The role of these other cereals – known generically as adjuncts – varies but can cover anything from making the beer darker to developing different flavours or simply helping to create a better foam.

The role of adjuncts has been decried over the years because of the way they have been employed by some very large breweries as a cost-cutting measure. By using a cheaper cereal than malted barley, they can shave pennies off the cost of a brew, which become millions of pounds or dollars when multiplied by the number of pints such enormous breweries produce. But, by using cheaper ingredients, these brewers also compromise the taste of their beers. In recent times, however, the role of adjuncts has gained a better understanding among beer connoisseurs who recognize the fact that sometimes they actually enhance a beer, or produce a desired effect which barley malt alone cannot achieve.

Simple barley, which has not been malted, is itself classed as an adjunct. It can be used roasted or flaked. Roasted barley is barley that has been kilned without undergoing the malting process. It produces well-roasted, bitter flavours and strong biscuit notes. Flaked barley is soaked and heat-treated at the maltings so that the starches released gelatinize and, with the help of enzymes from a base malt such as pale malt, can be easily absorbed into the mash and converted to sugars. A brewer may use flaked barley to develop a creamier, grainier beer or, thanks to its high protein content, to aid head retention.

Also classed as adjuncts are sugar and honey, which are often included in a beer to help raise the strength without adding to the body or the malt flavours. Apart from sugar, the most widely used adjunct is wheat, which in some cases can make up more than 50% of the cereal content, but is often used by brewers in small quantities to just lighten the flavour and colour of a beer and to help with head retention. Other common adjuncts are rice, maize (sometimes in the form of corn syrup), oats and rye.

Technicalities

Note that most adjuncts, used on their own, could not produce a viable wort for fermentation because they lack the vital enzymes that, in the case of barley, convert the grain's starches into fermentable sugars. Consequently, even beers with a high alternative cereal content still need malted barley in the mash so its enzymes can convert the starches into sugars. Some large breweries have separate cereal cookers which are used to boil the cereals first, to gelatinize their starches so that they can be converted into sugars by malted barley enzymes later in the mash.

TASTE OFF!

Adjuncts

To help identify the characteristics of the use of adjuncts, try this three-beer taste test. Each beer has a good percentage of one adjunct.

Asahi Super Dry (rice)

Note the paleness of colour, dryness of the palate, the lightness of body and the reined-back malt flavours. Overall, this makes it an easy-drinking, slender beer for the strength.

Suthwyk Palmerston's Folly (wheat)

Forty per cent of the cereal content of this beer is wheat, as evidenced in the crisp, delicate texture and straw colour. The subtlety of the cereal, with its absence of deep malt flavours, allows softly spicy, lemon and floral notes from the Saaz and Savinjski Golding hops to shine through.

Alechemy Rye O'Rye (rye)

This beer is dominated by the creamy, nutty, spicy characteristics of rye. Unlike in some rye beers, hops do not cloud the issue here: they add balancing bitterness but leave centre stage to the bold rye flavours, at least until the tangy finish.

Sugar

Sugar is not classed as an adjunct by some brewers, because it doesn't need to be converted for fermentation by enzymes. As its name suggests, the sugar in sugar is already available for the yeast to work with.

For brewing, sugar can be either produced from cane or beet – the end product, sucrose, is the same. However, brewers often like to use what is known as invert sugar. This is sugar in which the sucrose has been inverted, or broken down, to its basic components, glucose and fructose. Both of these are attacked eagerly by yeast, leaving very little residual sugar when the yeast has finished its work. The lack of residual sugar means less body in the beer, so a beer made entirely from sugar would be very thin. Consequently, sugar is used to supplement malted barley rather than replace it completely. Brewers generally add it to the copper boil, to raise strength but to keep the beer relatively slender, producing plenty of alcohol without overloading the palate with body and barley flavours. A great example of the use of sugar can be found in Belgium, where many beers – including those brewed by Trappist monks – incorporate a type of invert sugar known as candi sugar. This explains why some of the strongest beers in the world remain light and drinkable instead of turning out heavy and cloying. Burnt sugar – commonly known as caramel – is also sometimes added as a colouring, to darken a beer. Some milds were once made by simply darkening a light ale with caramel, although the more common practice today is to use darker malts to brew a proper mild.

Read on

Stan Hieronymus, *Brewing with Wheat* (Brewers Publications, 2010)

Wheat

Wheat *(Triticum aestivum)* is a similar grain to barley, except for two key points of importance as far as the brewer is concerned. Firstly, it has a lower natural enzyme activity, meaning it doesn't easily convert its own starches into fermentable sugars, and so barley needs to be used alongside it. This is the case even in wheat beers such as the German weizen where the mash can contain more than 50% wheat; for other beers, brewers will sometimes use wheat in small quantities to simply lighten the flavour, add a little refreshing acidity or help with foam creation, because of its good protein content. Secondly, wheat kernels do not have a husk, which leads to problems at the maltings and in the brewhouse.

Wheat can be used in malted or unmalted forms, because the starches can be freed for use in both cases, but some brewers (notably German weizen brewers) insist upon malted wheat. During the malting process, the grains soak up water much faster than barley grains, because there is no husk, and they can also clump together while germinating or in the kiln for the same reason. At the brewery, the lack of a husk would cause problems in the mash if the brewer did not also include malted barley. Wheat alone would degenerate into a sticky mess and there would be no natural filter bed created from husks through which the wort could be strained, leading to blocked pipes.

Brewers who favour using unmalted wheat in their beers often have to subject the cereal to a more rigorous mashing regime in order to free up starches from the harder grains.

Wheat can also be used by a brewer in other formats. Common is torrefied wheat, used for head retention. This is grain that has been heated to the point where it blows open, just like popcorn. This heat treatment gelatinizes the starches so that they can easily be accessed and converted in the mash.

Mashing

Once brewers have made their selection of malts and/or adjuncts, the mixture of grains (known as the grist) is passed through a mill to crack open the husks and endosperms and expose the starches. It is important not to overcrush the grains as the husks need to remain large enough to work as a filter in the mash tun. Some smaller breweries buy their grain pre-crushed while others reckon crushing on site provides a fresher grain character.

The grain is then fed into the mash tun at the same time as hot water is added. The optimum temperature for starch conversion is 65°C (149°F) but the water at this stage is slightly warmer, at around 75°C (167°F), because the coldness of the grain will bring down the temperature. Also important at this stage is the way in which the grain and water are fused together. In order to avoid clumps of grain, and to guarantee the correct temperature when it hits the mash tun, the cereal is fed in in regulated quantities, allowing the grains to be soaked equally.

With a steady 65°C (149°F) achieved in the mash tun, the grains are allowed to soak for an hour or so, to allow the starches to seep into the water and be converted into sugars by the natural barley enzymes. The mash is finished when conversion of starches to sugars is complete. Brewers check this either visually, by analysing the clarity of the mash tun liquid (wort), or by a litmus-type test in which a sample of the wort is dosed with iodine, which turns dark blue if starches are still present. It is important not to allow the mash to continue beyond this point, as tannins in the grains will increase in the wort, making it astringent. To end the mash, more hot water is added to raise the temperature to a level

Mashing extracts sugars from the grains, creating sweet wort

where the enzymes are destroyed and starch conversion comes to an end. At this point the wort is run off. Taps are opened to allow the liquid to filter down through the bed of grains, drawing out the last of the fermentable sugars. The grains in turn help to clarify the wort as it runs out, trapping larger solids. To wash out any remaining sugars, the bed of cereals is then sprayed with fresh hot water (around 75ºC/167ºF) from a rotating arm. This process is known as sparging.

Different brewing traditions use different mashing techniques

Technicalities

The sugars created during mashing are primarily of three types: glucose, maltose (composed of two linked glucose molecules) and maltotriose (composed of three linked glucose molecules). All are fully fermentable by brewer's yeast and therefore are intrinsic to the alcohol content of the finished beer. Also present are dextrins, types of glucose that cannot be fermented by brewer's yeast and so remain uneaten, giving more substance, or body, to a beer. The process of converting starches into sugars in this way is known as saccharification. Also as part of the mashing process, proteins extracted from the malt are rendered soluble, giving body (as well as foam) to the finished beer.

The description thus far provided of the mashing process relates largely to what is known as infusion mashing, common to ale breweries. Other brewing traditions follow different mashing processes. Many lager breweries still opt for the decoction system, in which thick, grain-heavy portions of the mash are removed from the mash mixer (as the mash tun is known in such breweries) and placed in a separate unit (a mash cooker) to be boiled for a while. This process breaks down cell walls in the malt, freeing up starches. A typical decoction mash begins at around 45ºC (113ºF), during which enzymes release starches from the endosperm and break down proteins into smaller units. Then the temperature rises to around 65ºC (149ºF) with the return of the boiling liquid from the mash cooker and the conversion of starches to sugars takes place. Because the more liquid parts of the mash are not extracted and boiled, enzymes are not damaged and can perform their functions, but some drinkers reckon they can detect a toasted note in the beer as a result of this boiling. The reason for such a complex mashing regime is historic, stemming back to the days when not all malt was as thoroughly prepared for brewing as today. The grain was 'under modified', meaning that it needed more vigorous heat treatment to free the starches. Some breweries use a third system, in which the mash remains in one vessel but the temperature is raised gradually from a starting point of around 45ºC (113ºF), allowing periods of rest (stands) after each temperature increase. The process is known as temperature-programmed mashing, or step mashing, and the stands permit various enzymes to work their magic at their ideal temperatures.

In many breweries, particularly those using decoction or temperature-programmed mashing, a separate vessel called a lauter tun is employed at the brewery, between the mash mixer and the copper. When mashing has finished, wort is pumped out of the mash mixer into the lauter tun for sparging and straining, leaving the mash mixer free for a new mash and hence adding capacity and turnover to a brewery. Also, because the lauter tun is wider and shallower than a typical mash tun/mash mixer, and the grains are more spread out, better sugar extraction can be achieved, especially with built-in rakes available to loosen compacted grains. The clarity of the wort is also improved by pumping wort run-off from the lauter tun back in on top of the grain bed and allowing it to filter again.

The mash tun

The mash tun is a relatively simple vessel, essentially just a large tub commonly made of stainless steel or copper. Malt and hot water enter at the top – sometimes using an old-fashioned grain and water mixing device known as a Steel's masher that ensures the right quantities of each enter at the same time – and wort filters out at the bottom via slotted plates at the end of the mash. A stirring arm may be incorporated and there is also a rotating sparging arm above that sprays hot water on the grains as the wort is run off. There is often no heat control, apart from the ability to pump in extra hot water to raise the temperature, if necessary. For decoction and temperature-controlled mashes however, the mash tun (or mash mixer) has built in sensors and controls that allow the adjustment of temperature.

A rotating sparge arm *sprays hot water* on the grains

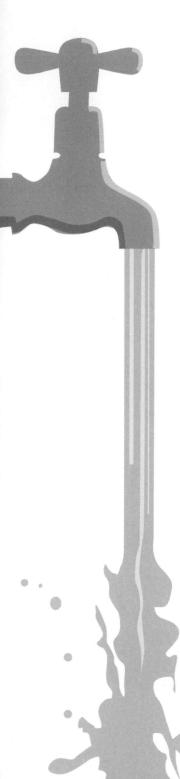

Water

In bar-room discussions about beer ingredients, water is often overlooked in favour of the headline grabbers, malt and hops. Considering that something like 95% of the contents of your pint is water, this is perhaps surprising.

One of the first things you learn on a brewery tour is that water used for brewing is not called that. It is called liquor. Water is the stuff that is used for cleaning the vessels and washing down the floor. Trade terminology aside, not all water/liquor is the same. Mineral and salt content – collected as water filters down through the rock strata of the Earth – varies enormously, making water hard or soft, or somewhere in between. Minerals and salts also influence the acidity of the water, which has an impact on the brewing process, enhancing or inhibiting the way malt and hop components are absorbed into the wort, for instance. They also have an impact on the way the yeast works and finally settles.

Some beers are best brewed using hard water and some using soft water. This is one reason why certain beer styles developed in precise geographical regions. However, today's technology means that water anywhere in the world can be adapted to brew any beer style, with salts added or removed as appropriate and the acidity of water adjusted. Breweries simply take their local water – perhaps from a spring, a bore hole, a lake or even just the mains water supply – and change the salt balance.

The first thing a brewer must establish, however, is the quality of the supply. Incoming water is checked for impurities and also for flavour defects, caused by contamination to the supply or changes made by the water supplier. Chlorine may be an issue and is removed to avoid developing medicinal flavours and aromas in the finished beer. Next the salt composition is adjusted. In some cases, brewers will strip out all the salts and then add those that are required.

Technicalities

To illustrate just how different brewing waters can be, you only have to compare the natural waters of Pilsen in the Czech Republic and Burton upon Trent in the UK. Pilsen's water has a total salts content of around 30 millivals (milligrams per litre), whereas Burton's water contains 1,226 millivals. The softer water of Pilsen led the town's brewers to develop the pilsner beer style, with its smooth mouthfeel and rich malt character, while the harder water of Burton was intrinsic to the production of the pale ale style, flinty and bright.

But it's not just the quantity of salts that matters: it's also the type of salts. Salts, in chemistry, are compounds resulting from the reaction of acids

TASTE OFF!

Water

All water tastes the same, doesn't it? Not really, not when you compare different examples, with varying mineral and salt contents. Pick up a few bottles of mineral water (ensure it's still water and not sparkling, so that the bubbles don't get in the way) and see for yourself. Check the labels and note the differing calcium, magnesium, sodium and chloride contents. See if you can identify any variations in flavour or texture. Saltiness may stand out in some, especially if the sodium and potassium content is high; others may taste a little sweeter if chloride levels are raised.

with alkalis or metals. Salts of calcium and magnesium, in the form of chlorides, bicarbonates and sulphates, are the main contributors to water hardness, with calcium sulphate (gypsum) the key hardness component that makes Burton ideal for pale ales. Its high concentration in the water assists in starch conversion, keeps protein haze low and helps prevent the wort from darkening during the boil. It also helps the integration of hop components, which is why Burton's pale ales have a crisp hop accent (although, because it is partly converted to hydrogen sulphide during fermentation, calcium sulphate can also lead to the development of an aroma of rotten eggs – known historically as the Burton snatch – when the beer is fresh). Brewers wishing to emulate the brewing water of Burton add calcium sulphate and also calcium chloride, which helps harden the water. This process is known as Burtonization.

Sodium and chloride salts are sweetness enhancers and good levels of these encourage the brewing of sweeter beer styles, such as mild or porter. London's water (totalling 463 millivals of salts) is relatively rich in sodium, hence the development of these styles in the UK capital. Also – like water in Dublin and Munich, for example – it is rich in calcium carbonate, which, with its natural alkalinity, helps balance the acidity found in dark malts – another factor in the city's historic preference for brewing dark beers.

Read on

John Palmer and Colin Kaminski, *Water: A Comprehensive Guide for Brewers* (Brewers Publications, 2013)

Insight

A brewer plans the strength of a beer primarily by controlling the amount of fermentable material put in at the start – in other words how much malt and other sugar-generating products are in the recipe. At the end of the mashing process, a reading is taken of the wort produced, using a device called a saccharometer or hydrometer – a kind of dipstick that floats higher or lower in the mash vessel, depending on the density of the wort (the denser the wort, the more dissolved solids – which are mostly sugars – it contains). The saccharometer reports its findings on a visible scale in a number of formats. These include specific gravity, which is commonly used in the UK. Before the wort is fermented, this is also known as the original gravity (OG). Water has a gravity of 1000 so a wort with an OG of, say, 1040, is 40 parts per thousand denser than water. As a rule of thumb, a wort with an OG of 1040 will result in a beer of around 4% alcohol by volume after fermentation. To make a stronger beer, the brewer needs to ensure the wort has a higher OG, and the opposite if a weaker beer is intended.

The saccharometer also shows its findings using a system known as degrees Plato, which is favoured in other countries. This is actually a weight-based system. A wort of 10° Plato contains 10 grammes of dissolved solids per 100 grammes of wort. To compare OGs and degrees Plato, simply multiply the Plato figure by four. Hence a beer of 10° Plato will have an OG of 1040.

If the wort is too dense for the beer planned, then the brewer can add more water to achieve the correct density. If it is too light, then sugar can be added for adjustment to the right level. The strength of a beer, however, is ultimately decided during fermentation and by the effectiveness of the yeast. The alcohol reading of the finished beer is most commonly declared as a percentage of the total liquid, and this is stated as the alcohol by volume (ABV) figure. This can be calculated by taking the OG figure and subtracting the final gravity figure (the reading after fermentation) and then applying various equations.

Hops

The hop is a plant that beer drinkers around the world hold dear, often without knowing very much about it. It's usually the first ingredient shouted out in response to the question 'What is beer made from?', when in fact the more obvious answer is barley. Hops, in essence, are a seasoning but they have some very useful properties beyond aroma and taste.

The hop is a tall, stringy plant that grows in twisting bines. Farmers cultivate it by training the bines to grow up poles and wires, enabling them to harvest the flowers that arrive at the end of summer. These flowers, almost like little green pine cones in appearance, with multiple layers of petals, are vital to the brewing process. Quickly dried (to prevent them deteriorating and to keep them usable for a year or more), they are shipped to breweries where they are added in various quantities, and at various times, to the boiling wort. The flowers bring balancing bitterness to the sweetness of the wort but also introduce a natural preservative, which helps keep the beer free from infection. Additionally, they provide a wide range of flavours.

Just as other plants, fruits and vegetables come in numerous varieties, with differing aromas and flavours (think different types of apples or tomatoes), so hop flavours and aromas differ by variety. The Target hop, for instance, while it can provide interesting marmalade notes if used judiciously, is generally known for its smooth bitterness, ideal for the profile of a British bitter. The Saaz hop has a mellow herbal quality, wonderful when used to its best in a classic pilsner. Golding, on the other hand, has a subtle citrus quality, although nothing like as pronounced as the radiant grapefruit, lemon and orange notes of American hops such as Cascade and Citra. Consequently, a brewer will often mix and match hops to achieve the desired aroma and flavour.

Less expressive hops – known as bittering hops – tend to be added to the copper boil early. They can then provide important bitterness but do not have much character to lose as the boil continues and steam and hop aromas disappear up the chimney. Later in the boil, perhaps just 10 minutes before it ends, so-called aroma hops – the more flamboyant varieties – are added, without the danger of their wonderful flavours and aromas being boiled away. Brewers will often add hops later in the process, too, such as in the fermentation tank, in a conditioning tank as the beer is maturing, or even to a cask containing finished beer, just to accentuate the hop profile of the beer. This process is known as dry hopping. Some hops are used for both bittering and aroma, and are known as dual-purpose hops.

Hands on ✋

To understand the true character of hops, drop into a home-brewing shop or book a tour of your local microbrewery. These will often allow you a few handfuls of assorted hop varieties to inspect. Take some cones of each variety at a time and crush them in your palms, rubbing your hands together to release the oils and resins. Take a few sharp sniffs of the aroma and begin to identify the differing qualities of each variety.

TASTE OFF!

Hops

A number of breweries now produce a single-hop beer – a beer that features just one variety of hop and can therefore be sampled to gain some idea of its aroma and flavour possibilities. Some even produce a range of single-hop beers, occasionally with the malt make-up and the strength set as standard and just the hop variety changing. Marston's Single-Hop series of monthly beers has been one such initiative and Marks & Spencer has also retailed a collection of single-hop beers. The ultimate hop flavour in the glass, however, depends on how, and in what quantities, the brewer has used the hop when making the beer, but tasting single-hop beers certainly provides a useful starting point for appreciation of hop character.

Coniston Bluebird Bitter (Challenger)

In many ways, this is a simple beer. It's just made from pale and crystal malts, with a single hop, Challenger. Challenger is normally used just for bittering but here it has a dual function, revealing just how much character the hop does have. Spicy grapefruit, orange and floral notes run right through the beer, from aroma to finish.

Hepworth Marks & Spencer Sussex Golden Ale (Golding)

This refreshing beer nicely exhibits the widely admired, rather delicate qualities of the Golding hop, offering leafy, gently earthy and woody notes, a little floral character and a lemon-orange fruitiness.

Oakham Citra (Citra)

American hops drive through this bright golden beer. Zesty oranges, grapefruit and passion fruit lead the way, with floral and pine notes also delivered by the Citra hops.

If you want to try more...

... try these other examples:
Buxton Moor Top (Chinook), Fuller's Bengal Lancer (Golding), Hop Back Summer Lightning (Golding), Oldershaw Caskade (Cascade), Pitfield Eco Warrior (Hallertauer Tradition), Stonehouse KPA (Green Bullet)

Technicalities

The Latin name of the hop is *Humulus lupulus*, the second word being Latin for small wolf, and reflecting the voracious way the plant takes over its breeding ground. It grows in temperate zones, in geographical bands between approximately 30° and 52° latitude, in both northern and southern hemispheres, where the temperature, rainfall and sun exposure are optimum. The major hop-growing countries are Germany, Czech Republic, Slovenia, Belgium, UK and the US in the northern hemisphere, and Australia and New Zealand in the southern hemisphere.

Hop bines grow quickly, twirling around anything that will provide support. Farmers train these bines along wires and poles, for ease of harvesting, and they can grow to a height of more than six metres (20 feet). After harvesting, when the bines are chopped down and the cones removed, the hop plants die away, only to grow back the following year. In the 1990s, much effort was put into breeding strains of hop that grow less high (below three metres/10 feet), so that they are easier to control for pests or diseases and simpler to harvest. These dwarf or hedgerow hops are best represented by the varieties First Gold, Pioneer, Boadicea and Sovereign.

Visit

Getting a close look at hops during cultivation is not easy. Farmers are extremely cautious about welcoming visitors who, they fear, may bring with them crippling diseases such as verticillium wilt, which has wiped out many thousands of acres of hops around the world. Only specially selected groups are occasionally allowed onto hop farmland – provided they have disinfected their footwear first. However, it is not impossible to see hops in the field, with places such as the National Trust's **Scotney Castle** (www.nationaltrust.org.uk/scotney-castle) in Kent, with its hop garden, open to the public.

Inside a hop flower

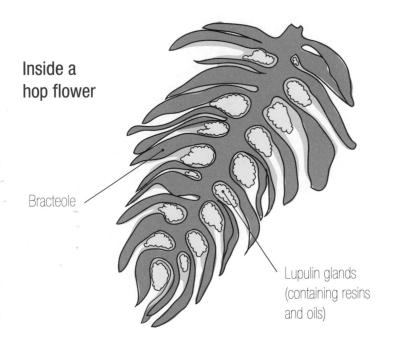

Bracteole

Lupulin glands (containing resins and oils)

In the UK, *hops* were traditionally dried in *oast houses*

The parts of the hop of interest to the brewer are the flowers, or cones. The petals of the cones are known as bracteoles and at the base of the bracteoles are glands that produce a sticky, yellow substance called lupulin, which is where the oils and resins vital for brewing are found.

The most recognized constituents of these resins are alpha acids (and, in particular, the alpha acid humulone), which provide bitterness. The higher the alpha acid content, the greater the potential bitterness in a beer. A higher alpha hop therefore can be used in smaller quantities than a lower alpha hop – a popular choice among big breweries that want to save money on hop costs. Unfortunately, the best aromas and flavours generally derive from lower alpha hops, so brewers will often use the two in conjunction, high alpha for bittering and lower alpha for aroma.

A calculation made by considering the known alpha acid content of a hop and the quantity of hops used can provide an indication of the potential bitterness of the finished beer. The figures that result are known as IBUs (International Bitterness Units), but a high IBU does not necessarily mean that the beer will be unduly bitter, as the character, richness and sweetness of the malt, and the strength of the beer, may offset some of the bitterness.

During brewing, alpha acid bitterness is extracted from the hops when they are boiled. Also extracted are beta acids (lupulones), which provide preservative qualities by fighting against certain bacteria and are responsible for essential oils that contribute to the flavour of beer. These oils bring the fruity, floral, spicy, herbal and other attributes identified earlier.

While hop plants are dioecious, meaning that they come in both male and female varieties, only female, seedless cones are used for brewing as male cones are smaller and less bountiful in oils and resins. Male hops are ruthlessly grubbed up in many parts of the world in order to prevent fertilization of the female plants which, brewers claim, can make their flavours too aggressive and coarse (hop plants do not require fertilization to propagate, farmers simply take and plant cuttings from existing plants).

Insight

Once a year, some brewers like to use what are known as green or wet hops. These are freshly harvested, whole-leaf hops that are rushed from the hop gardens and thrown into the copper without being pre-dried. Special beers produced in this way may also include conventional dried hops but they have a notably sappy, juicy hop character from the moisture-heavy new crop.

Read on

Stan Hieronymus, *For the Love of Hops* (Brewers Publications, 2012)

British Hop Association (www.britishhops.org.uk)

Hop Growers of America (usahops.org)

Hop Growers Union of the Czech Republic (czhops.cz)

The most common hop varieties

The following table summarizes the usage and flavours of the most popular hops. Bear in mind, however, that most are used in conjunction with one or more other hop variety and so the end result may be rather different. Alpha acid percentages are only approximate, as variations occur between harvests.

Hop	Country	Alpha acid	Main uses	Broad flavours
Admiral	UK	14.8	British ales; bittering	Citrus
Ahtanum	US	5.7	American ales; aroma	Floral, spicy
Amarillo	US	8.5	American ales; bittering	Tropical fruit, citrus
Aurora	Slovenia	8.2	American/British ales; aroma	Floral, pine
Bobek	Slovenia	5.2	American/British ales; aroma	Floral, pine
Bramling Cross	UK	6.9	British ales; aroma	Blackcurrant, citrus
Brewer's Gold	Germany/US	9.0	German lagers; bittering	Citrus
Cascade	US	5.5	American ales; aroma	Citrus, pine
Celeia	Slovenia	5.2	British ales; aroma	Floral, citrus
Centennial	US	10.5	American ales; bittering	Floral, citrus
Challenger	UK	7.5	British ales; bittering	Peppery, citrus
Chinook	US	13.0	American ales; bittering	Citrus, pine
Citra	US	12.0	American ales; bittering	Citrus
Cluster	US	7.0	American ales/stouts; bittering	Floral, spicy
Columbus	US	15.0	American ales; bittering	Herbal, citrus
Crystal	US	4.5	American ales; aroma	Floral, spicy
First Gold	UK	7.0	British ales; bittering/aroma	Fruity, floral
Fuggle	UK	4.5	British ales; bittering	Tropical fruit
Galaxy	Australia	13.5	American/British ales; aroma	Tropical fruit, citrus
Galena	US	13.0	American ales; bittering	Floral, citrus
Golding	UK	5.5	British ales; aroma	Citrus, tea
Green Bullet	New Zealand	12.5	Lagers; bittering	Herbal, floral, fruity
Hallertauer Hersbrucker	Germany	4.5	German lagers; aroma	Herbal
Hallertauer Magnum	Germany	13.5	German lagers; bittering	Herbal, floral

Hop	Country	Alpha acid	Main uses	Broad flavours
Hallertauer Mittelfrüh	Germany	4.5	German lagers; aroma	Herbal
Liberty	US	4.0	American lagers; aroma	Herbal
Mosaic	US	12.5	American ales; aroma	Tropical fruit
Motueka	New Zealand	7.5	American/British ales; aroma	Tropical fruit, citrus
Mount Hood	US	6.0	American lagers; aroma	Herbal
Nelson Sauvin	New Zealand	12.5	American ales; bittering/aroma	Fruity, winey
Northdown	UK	8.0	British ales; bittering	Grassy
Northern Brewer	UK/US	8.0	British/American ales; bittering	Grassy
Nugget	US	13.0	American ales; bittering	Herbal
Pacific Gem	New Zealand	15.0	New Zealand ales; bittering	Tropical fruit
Perle	US/Germany	8.0	American ales/German lagers; bittering	Herbal
Pioneer	UK	9.0	British ales; bittering	Citrus
Pride of Ringwood	Australia	10.0	Australian lagers; bittering	Citrus
Progress	UK	6.5	British ales; aroma	Herbal, floral
Saaz	Czech Republic	3.5	Pilsners; bittering/aroma	Herbal
Savinjski Golding	Slovenia	5.0	British ales; aroma	Floral, elderflower
Simcoe	US	13.0	American ales; bittering	Citrus, pine
Sorachi Ace	US	13.0	American ales/saisons; bittering/aroma	Citrus, herbal
Sovereign	UK	5.5	British ales; bittering	Herbal, floral
Spalt	Germany	4.0	German lagers; aroma	Herbal, floral
Sterling	US	7.5	American ales; aroma	Herbal, citrus
Target	UK	11.0	British ales; bittering	Citrus
Tettnanger	Germany	4.5	German lagers; aroma	Floral, herbal
Willamette	US	5.0	American ales; bittering	Spicy

Visit

The following centres and events offer lots of fascinating information about hops and their history.

American Hop Museum, Toppenish, Washington, USA (americanhopmuseum.org)

Faversham Hop Festival, Kent (favershamhopfestival.org)

German Hop Museum, Wolnzach, Germany (hopfenmuseum.de)

Hop & Beer Temple, Žatec, Czech Republic (chchp.cz)

Kent Life, Sandling, Kent (www.kentlife.org.uk)

Poperinge Hop Museum, Poperinge, Belgium (hopmuseum.be)

Hops are available in several forms to brewers. The first is whole leaf – simply hop flowers that have been dried from around 80% humidity after picking to around 10%, to prevent deterioration. In the UK, this originally took place in distinctive oast houses – round structures with a conical top. After drying in the hot air of a kiln for about 10 hours, the hops are compressed to eliminate oxygen (and prevent staling) and packed into giant sacks, known as pockets. At the brewery, the leaves need to be strained out from the hopped wort at the end of the boil and this is done by diverting the contents of the copper through a vessel called the hop back (some hops are actually added here to give a late burst of aroma and flavour to the wort as it is run off).

The second option for brewers are pellet hops – hops that have been crushed and compacted into pellets soon after picking. The advantage of pellets, which are packed into smaller, vacuum-sealed units, is a longer shelf life, but they also need different equipment in the brewhouse. The powdery debris they leave behind in the copper cannot be captured by the hop back and so a centrifuge or whirlpool is employed to separate it from the wort.

The third option is hop oil – the essence of hops extracted into a liquid. This is a popular choice to augment whole or pellet hops in Germany, and also among large, multi-national brewers.

Herbs, spices and fruit

Before hops became widely used in brewing in the 15th century, herbs and spices acted as preservative and bitterness providers. These were used sometimes individually, at other times in a mixture known as gruit, and added to the boil. Commonly found in gruit were bog myrtle (also known as sweet gale), wild rosemary and yarrow, but many other herbs and spices were also called into service. In Scandinavia and the Baltic countries juniper was a common flavouring (using both twigs and berries in the copper); in Scotland, heather was used. Some of these old-style beers have been resurrected by adventurous brewers, and herbs and spices are also now used individually, the most common being ginger and coriander (the latter particularly in Belgian wheat beers). Sage, lemon grass, vanilla, elderflower, liquorice and chilli also feature in some beers. Various fruits are used in brewing, too. Their role is often just to add fruit flavour but in some cases the fruit – added after the boil – also contributes to the fermentation, bringing its own sugars and even wild yeasts. More about this practice can be found in the section on lambics, but among the fruits commonly seen in beer are cherries, raspberries and damsons.

The boil

When wort arrives in the copper from the mash tun or lauter tun it is still warm but far from boiling. The heat in the copper is turned up and the wort eventually begins to boil. A rolling boil is then maintained, allowing sterilization of the wort, the termination of enzymic activity that might create more sugar from starches, and the release of bitterness from the hops into the wort. The boiling also slightly darkens the wort by caramelizing some of the sugars and it causes proteins to clump together and settle out. These isolated proteins, along with the spent hops, are collectively known as trub and this is removed by running the wort into a vessel known as a hop back (for whole-leaf hopped beer) or a centrifuge or whirlpool (for pellet-hop beer). The whole boiling process generally takes between one and one-and-a-half hours, but sometimes longer boils are required to evaporate more of the wort, thus increasing the concentration of sugars, in order to make a stronger beer.

Technicalities

The release of bitterness from hops is caused by boiling and, chemically, involves the conversion of alpha acids in the hops into iso-alpha acids. This process is known as isomerization. The initial clumping together of proteins during the boil is known as the hot break. More proteins settle out later, as the wort begins to cool in the copper, and this stage is called the cold break. The removal of these proteins clarifies the beer and the process is helped along by the addition of a substance known as copper finings, or Irish moss (in fact an extract from a dried seaweed called carrageen). This is added just before the wort is run off and works because its negatively charged molecules attract positively charged molecules of protein, rendering them insoluble.

In the hop back, the spent hops that settle on the bottom plate act as a filter and capture the settled-out proteins. If, instead, a centrifuge or whirlpool is used, the wort is spun around to separate the hops and proteins from the liquid for easy removal.

The copper

The copper is perhaps more correctly referred to as the kettle. This is because not many of these vessels are made from copper these days. Copper became a popular choice for kettle manufacturing for a number of reasons, including its malleability – the way it is easily shaped – which led to the graceful onion-dome appearance of the classic kettle. Also of importance was copper's heat conductivity, giving it the edge over iron, for example. Today, most 'coppers' are actually made of stainless steel.

Traditionally, coppers were heated by direct flame, with wood or coal burning beneath. The modern choice is steam, which is passed through pipes immersed in the wort or lining the walls of the copper. It is a much more efficient

Insight 🔍

Traditionally, wort cooling was conducted in large open trays, known as coolships, with the large surface area helping the air lower the temperature of the wort. During this procedure, however, wild yeasts and other bacteria could enter the wort. For most modern brewers that would be unacceptable, but the old system is still used in some breweries, particularly in Belgium, where the wild organisms are important in the production of lambic beer.

method of heating and is less likely to concentrate heat in a few places, which can lead to caramelization of the wort and a burnt flavour. Some small breweries use electric elements to heat the wort.

The copper often has an internal heating column called a calandria, through which the boiling wort is vigorously circulated. Calandrias can also be external, with the wort pumped to and from the copper to be heated. Most coppers today are totally enclosed (a huge safety plus), but with a chimney at the top to allow the escape of steam. It is in the copper that additional sugars are often added as well as hops.

On leaving the copper, the wort is cooled using a heat exchanger, a radiator-like device in which plates filled with cold water alternate with plates containing the hot wort. The cold water picks up heat (and is then recycled in the brewery, thus saving energy), while the wort loses heat. The wort needs to be lowered to around 18°C (64°F), if an ale is being brewed, or around 11°C (52°F) for a lager.

Yeast

Yeast is a single-celled fungus that is responsible for fermentation, although for millennia brewers didn't understand that. They recognized that the foam that naturally built up on top of a beer seemed to have magical properties, that it could be removed and used to make another beer, but they didn't know what it was. So bemused were they that they just named it godisgood. It was only in the 19th century that brewers and scientists really got to grips with what yeast was and what it does: in short, when yeast encounters sugars, it eats them and expels in their place carbon dioxide and alcohol.

While brewers once used yeasts that exist wild in the atmosphere, today brewing yeasts have been specially selected and cultured for the best results, with different strains of yeast used for the type of beer being brewed. Yeast used for making ale, for instance, tends to sit on the top of the fermenting wort and functions at a warmer temperature than lager yeast, which tends to drop to the bottom although, with changes to fermentation equipment and practices, the clear demarcation between top- and bottom-fermenting yeasts has become blurred. Within both ale and lager yeast families there are many individual strains of yeast. Then there are also wild yeasts that are still used to ferment certain beer styles, such as lambic.

Brewers cherish and protect the strains of yeast they know deliver consistent results. Often, they have been using these for decades and know that, if they had to replace their yeast with another strain, their beers might not ferment

Brewing yeasts are carefully selected and cultivated by brewers

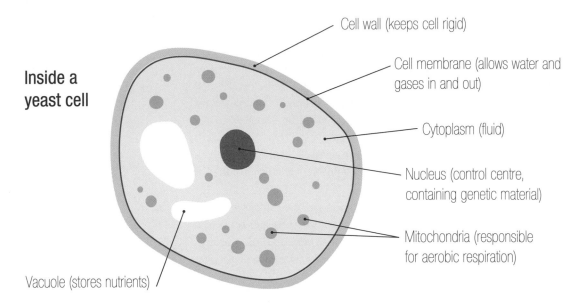

Inside a yeast cell

Cell wall (keeps cell rigid)

Cell membrane (allows water and gases in and out)

Cytoplasm (fluid)

Nucleus (control centre, containing genetic material)

Mitochondria (responsible for aerobic respiration)

Vacuole (stores nutrients)

in the same way, leading to variations in flavour or even greater problems. Consequently, most breweries lodge samples of their yeasts in special yeast banks, from which they can be retrieved if there is a catastrophe at the brewery and the yeast is infected or destroyed. Similarly, many brewers will not allow a different yeast strain into their brewhouses, for fear it will contaminate their own yeast and cause problems.

As well as creating alcohol and carbon dioxide from sugar, yeasts produce a myriad of other, mostly subtle, flavour notes from their ingestion of proteins and other components of the wort, helping to create the overall flavour that makes each beer individual and different. Some yeasts, particularly ale yeasts, are also prone to creating esters, particularly when the strength of the beer rises to around 5% ABV and above. Esters are chemical compounds that are also found in plants and fruits, so it's not surprising to find beers that have aromas and flavours similar to tropical fruits and flowers. To keep the creation of esters to a low level, brewers will ensure the fermentation temperature does not get too high. Other brewers, conversely, actively seek such exotic flavours in certain beers and so encourage the production of esters by choosing yeasts that are known for their ester creation. A good example of this approach is the German weizen, which is known for its banana and apple flavours.

On the downside, yeast can also create other compounds, most of which are undesirable. These include fusel alcohols, which taste warm and solvent-like, and are considered by some to be responsible for hangover headaches; diacetyl, a butterscotch note that is accepted in small doses in a few beer styles but disliked in others; organic acids that, if present in too great a quantity, can resemble vinegar, farmyards and even, sorry to say, vomit; sulphur notes, varying from a struck match to rotten eggs; and phenolic compounds, which contribute medicinal, clove, smoky and plastic-like notes. Most of these unwanted results are eradicated through skilful brewing.

Technicalities

Brewer's yeast belongs to the genus *Saccharomyces*, meaning sugar fungus. Within the genus *Saccharomyces* are species such as *Saccharomyces cerevisiae* and *Saccharomyces pastorianus*. *Saccharomyces cerevisiae* is known as ale yeast, and it is not as efficient as other types of yeast. It leaves behind some unfermented sugars and is more prone to ester production. This, combined with the warmer temperature at which it works best, results in ale being fruitier and more complex than lager. Lager yeast, *Saccharomyces pastorianus* – named after scientist Louis Pasteur, whose experiments significantly improved brewers' knowledge of yeast – was previously known as *Saccharomyces carlsbergensis* as it was isolated and selected by scientist Emil Christian Hansen at Carlsberg's brewery in Copenhagen, although it is in fact a derivation of a yeast first used in Bavaria, Germany. There, brewers noticed that beer stored in icy caves remained drinkable throughout a hot summer, not realizing that this was probably because wild yeasts and other infections in the open air struggled to survive in the chilly, subterranean environment. During its cold storage, the yeast in the beer sank to the bottom and remained relatively pure, not suffering the infections and cross-breeding endured by ale yeast that, in other places, sat on the top of fermenting wort. Hansen took this purer yeast and, building on work by Pasteur, honed it to perfection, removing other corrupting yeast strains and infections. His efforts ensured beer remained drinkable for longer.

All the above relates to yeasts that have been harnessed for brewing, but some forms of beer are fermented using wild yeasts. The best-known of these yeasts is a genus called *Brettanomyces*, meaning the British yeast. It is thought it was commonly found in aged British ales at one time, giving the beer an infected off-flavour. Today, it is best known for its use by Belgian brewers who make wild yeast beers (see Lambics). For these, *Brettanomyces* living naturally in the atmosphere settles in the wort as it cools and starts to work once *Saccharomyces* yeasts, which also find their way into the beer, have run their course. Over several weeks, if not months, the *Brettanomyces* eats up more sugars and introduces its own distinctive spicy, earthy notes to the beer. Many adventurous brewers around the world now create unusual beers by injecting *Brettanomyces* into their products.

Some forms of beer are fermented using wild yeasts

Fermentation

The process of adding yeast to wort in order to begin fermentation is known as pitching. Cooled to the appropriate temperature, the wort is transferred into a fermentation vessel. In its simplest form, this is a deep tub made of stone or metal (usually stainless steel today), with inlets and outlets to allow the passage of wort in and, eventually, beer out. Many vessels are now fully enclosed. This brings several advantages, including better hygiene and the chance to install automatic cleaning systems, but brewers of certain styles, such as ales and wheat beers, often prefer the open system, claiming the access to oxygen, the shallowness of the vessel, the way the yeast settles and other factors all help add character to the beer. That said, enclosed, tall, cylindroconical vessels are now in use at many breweries and are employed for both ale and lager production. These are efficient to use, occupy less floor space, and their temperature is more easily controlled. One further important benefit is that the shape of these vessels encourages the yeast to sink to the bottom, from where it can be easily extracted. Even certain ale yeasts can conform, instead of sitting, as traditional ones do, on the top.

The quantity of yeast pitched varies according to the style of beer, with lager beers needing more yeast. Air is pumped in, to oxygenate the wort and feed the yeast, which now rouses itself from a relatively dormant phase into vigorous action. After taking a few hours to get used to its new environment, the yeast eagerly gets to work, taking advantage of the abundant sugars, minerals and vitamins to reproduce itself. In ale brewing, within a couple of days, a thick duvet of foam has developed on the top of the wort and the air is filled with fruity aromas; in lager brewing, the yeast tends to drop to the bottom instead, and reproduces less quickly. Heat is naturally generated by the fermentation process so the temperature of the wort increases, heading up to around 22°C (72°F) for ale and 14°C (57°F) for lager. To prevent the temperature rising higher, which would make the yeast less productive, the fermentation vessel generally has a cooling mechanism built in – often coils of cold water immersed in the wort.

After four or five days (up to two or three weeks for lager), the first stage of fermentation (primary fermentation) is over. The yeast has used up most of the sugars and begins to slow down. Most of the yeast is removed, leaving some in suspension in the wort – now called green beer – to continue a more relaxed fermentation. With most of the sugars eaten away, and the yeast itself rather tired, the fermentation is much more modest at this stage and serves to just mature, or condition, the beer, ensuring the rougher flavours are rounded off and that there is good, natural carbonation in the beer. This conditioning process often takes place in separate vessels, freeing up the fermentation tank for another brew. The yeast that has been removed is either cleaned for re-use, or sold to manufacturers of yeast extract products, such as Marmite and Vegemite, or makers of dietary supplements (yeast is rich in B vitamins). After packaging for distribution, unless the beer is filtered and/or pasteurized, the yeast continues to ferment sugars in the beer, producing a little more alcohol and carbon dioxide.

Technicalities

Yeast reproduces by dividing its cells. It does this rapidly in the presence of sugars and oxygen, hence the quickly generated head of yeast on the wort; this process is known as aerobic reproduction. Once the oxygen has been used up, yeast begins to work anaerobically. Reproduction is much slower and the rate of alcohol creation is also lower, meaning that the rest of the primary fermentation period is less aggressive. Throughout the period of fermentation, the yeast also absorbs minerals and other nutrients from the wort. These keep it in good health and able to finish the job.

After fermentation, some of the yeast is often reused at the brewery. It may be washed with acid to destroy any bacteria and is then repitched into a new batch of wort. This may happen several times, but the brewery will often then go back to the original yeast as, several brews down the line, the repitched yeast will slowly begin to mutate, with consequences for flavour. While it is common to talk about a particular brewery's yeast, in many cases this is composed of more than one strain of yeast which work compatibly with each other.

If a yeast fails to adequately ferment available sugars in the wort, the beer is said to be under-attenuated and leans, of course, toward the sweet side. If the opposite happens, and too many sugars are fermented away, the beer is over-attenuated and dry.

Fermentation times vary from beer to beer. Lager yeasts have been perfected to work more slowly than ale yeasts, enduring the lower fermentation temperature to gradually eat away at the sugars and dry out the beer. Primary fermentation may take a week or more longer than for an ale, and then follows a long period of cold conditioning, with temperatures set at around 0ºC (32ºF). Some breweries still allow up to three months for cold conditioning; others reckon a few weeks is enough. In some industrial-scale breweries the conditioning is much shorter again. This period of storage is known as lagering, after the German word meaning to store.

Read on

Chris White and Jamil Zainasheff, *Yeast: The Practical Guide to Beer Fermentation* (Brewers Publications, 2010)

Insight 🔍

Two particular types of fermentation vessels are historic to the UK. The first is the Burton Union System, currently only used by Marston's in Burton upon Trent. This system involves fermentation taking place in a series of large wooden casks, which are linked together (held in union) for easy filling with partially fermented wort that has been started off in more conventional vessels. From each cask, a swan-necked pipe rises to an overflow tray. As the wort ferments, the vigorous action of the yeast forces it up through the pipe into the tray, where excess yeast is left behind as the wort drops back into the cask to continue its fermentation. The second system is the Yorkshire square, still employed by Samuel Smith in Tadcaster and Black Sheep in Masham, for example. It operates in a similar way to the Burton Union System in that wort is pumped from the square-shaped fermentation vessel up into a false ceiling, where excess yeast is trapped as the wort is recycled back into the square below. The yeasts used in unions and squares are known to function well in such environments and one further benefit of both systems is that good-quality excess yeast is naturally filtered out for re-use.

Packaging

Following fermentation, the beer is packaged for distribution to customers. In the UK, the vast majority of ales are presented in cask-conditioned form. This means that they are run off into a container called a cask for delivery to the pub, allowing some of the living yeast to stay in the beer and continue maturing it. Sometimes a little extra sugar (known as priming), or sugar-rich partially fermented wort is added to ensure a good secondary fermentation. As a result, when you order a pint of this type of beer in a pub, it is still fermenting and conditioning. The beer is not filtered, pasteurized or artificially carbonated – the gentle effervescence in the beer is naturally produced by the yeast in the cask. This form of beer is also known as real ale and is usually served through handpumps on the bar.

The alternative to cask-conditioned beer is brewery-conditioned beer. This is beer that does not contain living yeast. The beer is chilled and filtered to remove all presence of yeast, and then pasteurized just in case any yeast happens to survive this rigorous (and often flavour-damaging) process. Because there is no active yeast in the beer, the beer has to be artificially carbonated to give it some life. Packaged in a pressurized container called a keg, it is forced from the keg to the bar by added carbon dioxide gas (sometimes mixed with nitrogen for a creamier character) when a tap is flicked open. Brewery-conditioned beer may have its benefits in being a long-life product, but most drinkers recognize that it fails to deliver the fresh, complex flavours of cask-conditioned beer.

The same principles apply to beer that is packaged in bottles or cans. Most bottled and canned beers are the equivalent of brewery-conditioned keg beer, in being filtered, pasteurized and artificially carbonated, but there are bottled (and indeed canned) equivalents of cask-conditioned draught beer, too. Bottle-conditioned (and can-conditioned) beers contain a small dosing of live yeast to ensure a natural carbonation and fresh flavours. However, the world of beer packaging is not as clear cut as it was only a decade or so ago, with many breweries now presenting keg, bottled and canned beers in a sort of halfway house format, often filtering the beer but stopping short of pasteurization.

Technicalities

The transfer of beer into a cask is known as racking. After leaving the fermentation vessel or a conditioning tank, the beer is temporarily held in a racking tank, which is linked to the filling apparatus. At this stage, priming sugar – to ensure a good secondary fermentation – and/or extra dry hops – for enhanced hop character – may be added. Casks, traditionally, were made of wood and some breweries still use oak casks but these are very rare. Most casks today are made of stainless steel, although recent times have seen the introduction of much cheaper plastic equivalents. Laid horizontally, the cask has a hole in the top, called a bunghole, and a hole in one end called the tap hole. The tap hole is closed with a wooden plug called a keystone before the cask is filled via the bunghole. Also added is a small amount of liquid finings – generally made from isinglass. Isinglass is derived from the swim bladder of certain tropical fish. Its role is to clarify the beer, its positive charge attracting the negatively charged yeast and dragging it to the bottom of the cask. Some brewers now prefer to omit finings, trusting their customers will not be concerned if the beer is a little hazy.

The casks are then stored at the brewery for a few days before delivery to pubs and bars, where they are positioned on a rack in a cool cellar and allowed to settle in a process known as stillaging. Before serving, each cask needs to be vented to allow some of the natural carbonation created by the yeast to be released. This is done again via the bunghole, which has been sealed using a wooden plug called a shive. In the centre of the shive, is a smaller section known as a tut. This can be knocked through into the cask to provide a vent, which is then plugged with a porous wooden peg called a spile. Some carbon dioxide

Read on

Patrick O'Neill,
Cellarmanship (CAMRA
Books, 2015)

can escape from the cask through the porous spile but, when carbonation starts to diminish, a non-porous spile can be used to provide a better seal and prevent further gas release.

Before going on sale, the cask needs to be tapped. This involves knocking a metal or plastic tap into the keystone on the end of the cask. Once the beer has settled again, and the sediment has dropped into the conveniently curved belly of the cask, below the tap hole, the tap can be turned to release the beer, which flows by gravity into the glass. Alternatively, a pipe can be fixed to the tap to allow the use of a handpump to draw the beer into the glass from further away. Sometimes an electric pump does the same job.

Casks come in various sizes, from the four-and-a-half imperial gallon pin, to the very common nine-gallon firkin, the less common 18-gallon kilderkin and the now rare 36-gallon barrel. Most cask-conditioned ales benefit from being stored and served at around 12ºC (54ºF) – i.e. cool, rather than cold. This keeps them fresh but avoids over-chilling that would mask complexity of the flavour they offer.

Assuming it is not exposed to extremes of temperature, an unvented cask of beer will remain in good, drinkable condition for at least a few weeks after leaving the brewery, although some beers benefit from being left longer; barley wines, for instance, are occasionally tucked away in a pub cellar for a year or more. However, after tapping, the beer begins to deteriorate, losing carbonation and gradually becoming stale and possibly sour, as beer is drawn off and air replaces it. For this reason it is highly recommended that the cask be consumed within three days of tapping. The life of cask beer can be prolonged by the use of a device called a cask breather, or aspirator. This allows carbon dioxide to enter the cask to fill the space vacated by drawn-off beer. The gas is applied at atmospheric pressure, to avoid over-saturating the beer with carbon dioxide, and this blanket of gas protects the beer from oxygen, which would hasten the staling process, and any airborne bacteria that may cause souring. Proponents consider the cask breather to be a useful ally in keeping beer drinkable in slow-turnover pubs; opponents (including CAMRA) consider that the longer sale period may lead to detrimental flavour changes in the beer and that its use may encourage the stocking of too many ales that may be drinkable but are not at their best.

The term racking also applies to the transfer of beer into pressurized kegs. Beer for kegging is often matured first at the brewery, to compensate a little for the lack of maturation once it leaves the brewery. The beer may sit in conditioning tanks for a couple of weeks before it is chilled, filtered and, very often, pasteurized. Chilling inhibits the yeast from working but the real impact comes from filtration, which strips out almost all the yeast cells to prevent further

The transfer of beer into a *cask* is known as *racking*

fermentation. There are a number of types of filters used in breweries, all working on the same principle – the beer is passed through a porous material that traps particles that are too big. Some filters are more efficient than others and are used accordingly by brewers that either want a rough filter, to remove just the bulk of yeast and unwanted proteins in order to improve clarity, or a rigorous filter in which the finest particles are removed. The latter, known as sterile or cold filtration, reduces elements that may cause spoilage in a beer designed for long-term sale (as in a bottle or can). The process may mean that pasteurization is not necessary. The downside is that the filtration is so efficient that it also removes particles that are responsible for colour, body, aroma and taste, resulting in a stripped-down beer. To compensate for this, some brewers brew slightly stronger or more heavily hopped versions of draught beers that are destined for bottling, so that, even if some flavour is lost during filtration, there is still plenty left.

The final step of processing beer for most kegs, bottles and cans is pasteurization. This involves heating the beer in order to kill off remaining yeast cells, bacteria and any other micro-organisms that may spoil it. The process is named after the French scientist Louis Pasteur, who identified that beer became spoiled because of such unwanted agents. Many brewers still doggedly cling to pasteurization even though it is widely considered that this heat treatment damages the taste of the beer, particularly that of pale and delicate beers. The process is also responsible for speeding up the staling process, by heating any oxygen present and hastening its reaction with various compounds in the beer. The resultant oxidation produces unpleasant papery notes.

Keg beer in the UK, since its introduction in the mid-20th century, has been mostly pasteurized. However, the new generation of keg beers that have arrived in the last few years take their lead from keg beer in the US, where it is mostly left unpasteurized. Unpasteurized keg beer needs to be kept chilled, in case unplanned refermentation begins. Consequently, keg beer – whether because it is of the old school and lacks good flavour, which is best disguised by chilling, or of the new school and needs to be kept fresh – is generally served colder than cask beer. Unpasteurized keg beer also has a modest shelf-life (up to around 60 days) whereas the pasteurized equivalent lasts longer.

The steel keg is basically a cylindrical tub without the graceful curves of a cask. There are no separate venting and tapping holes in a keg, just one inlet at the top (the keg is stood on end). The opening is accessed via a self-closing valve, using a coupling that allows gas (usually carbon dioxide but sometimes a mix of carbon dioxide and nitrogen) into the keg. The beer is forced by the gas up a central spear and into an affixed pipe that takes the beer to the bar. Like casks, kegs are made in various sizes, usually today in metric measures; for example

A new generation of keg beers is being left unpasteurized

20 litres (4.4 gallons), 30 litres (6.6 gallons) and 50 litres (11 gallons). In the US, kegs tend to be bigger and sized in multiples of US gallons.

Because gas is generally added to the container at the brewery (to ensure the lifeless beer is not flat) and then more gas is applied to force the beer to the bar, keg beer is usually much more saturated in carbon dioxide than cask beer. This makes the beer more prickly on the tongue and sometimes adds a sharp, acidic note, especially at low temperatures when even more carbon dioxide becomes dissolved.

When the gas applied is a mixture of nitrogen and carbon dioxide (at a ratio of around 70% nitrogen to 30% carbon dioxide for ales and stouts, and often 40% to 60% for lagers), the texture is softer, as the nitrogen does not dissolve so easily into the beer. Also, the smaller nitrogen bubbles create a thick, creamy head that lasts longer. This is the process that was originally developed to dispense Draught Guinness and is now applied to so-called nitro-keg beers, also known by proprietary terms such as Creamflow and Smoothflow. Some brewers believe it has a beneficial effect, particularly on darker keg beers, enhancing the creaminess; critics suggest the flattening effect of the gas creates a dull, rather characterless beer that lacks crispness.

TASTE OFF!

Carbon dioxide

To understand the impact of excess carbon dioxide in beer, do a simple taste test with two bottles of mineral water that are identical (same brand) apart from the fact that one is still and the other is carbonated. You should notice that the carbonated water not only has a livelier, more prickly texture but also a slightly acidic and sour note. This is because carbon dioxide has dissolved in the water and reacted with it, creating carbonic acid. The same happens with beer.

Visit

Many breweries (large and small) offer tours that explain and illustrate how beer is made and the importance of the various ingredients. Most need to be booked in advance and may be open only to groups of tourists, such as pub parties or CAMRA branches. However, there are some notable brewery tours for individuals available on a walk-in basis, or with just a little pre-booking; these include:

Adnams, Southwold, Suffolk (tours.adnams.co.uk)

Batemans, Wainfleet, Lincolnshire (bateman.co.uk)

Belhaven, Dunbar, East Lothian (www.belhaven.co.uk)

Black Sheep, Masham, North Yorkshire (www.blacksheepbrewery. com)

Fuller's, Chiswick, London (www. fullers.co.uk)

Greene King, Bury St Edmunds, Suffolk (greenekingshop.co.uk)

Hall & Woodhouse, Blandford Forum, Dorset (www.hall-woodhouse.co.uk)

Hook Norton, Hook Norton, Oxfordshire (www.hooky.co.uk)

Jennings, Cockermouth, Cumbria (www.jenningsbrewery.co.uk)

Marston's, Burton upon Trent, Staffordshire (www. marstonsbrewery.co.uk)

Meantime, Greenwich, London (meantimebrewing.com)

Palmers, Bridport, Dorset (palmersbrewery.com)

Rhymney, Blaenavon, Newport (rhymneybreweryltd.com)

Robinsons, Stockport, Greater Manchester (www. robinsonsvisitorscentre.co.uk)

St Austell, St Austell, Cornwall (www.staustellbrewery.co.uk)

Shepherd Neame, Faversham, Kent (www.shepherdneame.co.uk)

Theakston, Masham, North Yorkshire (www.theakstons.co.uk)

Wadworth, Devizes, Wiltshire (www. wadworthvisitorcentre.co.uk)

Wychwood, Witney, Oxfordshire (www.wychwood.co.uk)

Read on

John J Palmer, *How to Brew* (Brewers Publications, 2006)

Charlie Papazian, *The Complete Joy of Home Brewing* (William Morrow, 2014)

Graham Wheeler, *Home Brewing* (CAMRA Books, 1997)

American Homebrewers Association (www.homebrewersassociation.org)

Craft Brewing Association (www.craftbrewing.org.uk)

Brewlab in Sunderland runs *brewing courses* **for novice brewers**

Hands on

Home-brewing is an excellent way to further your understanding of beer. Many of the world's finest brewers began as home-brewers, perhaps even using the elementary starter kits that are widely on sale, and then progressing to using fresh malt and hops. Plenty of guidance is available for anyone thinking of following suit and there are numerous home-brewing clubs and societies that offer support and camaraderie. Home-brewing shops are also able to provide advice. There are also facilities such as Ubrew (www.ubrew.cc), a London-based 'open brewery' where you can learn the ropes from experienced brewers and create your own beer.

If you're really serious about getting into brewing, then opportunities are presented by the many small breweries that now exist. Job vacancies as cask washers or delivery drivers may open out into brewing itself for the right sort of enthusiastic candidate, with on-site training often augmented by formal brewing courses, leading to diplomas from the Institute of Brewing & Distilling (www.ibd.org.uk).

Alternatively, setting up your own brewery has become easier thanks to the development of learn-to-brew courses organized by Brewlab in Sunderland (www.brewlab.co.uk) and PBC (Brewery Installations) in Bury (pbcbreweryinstallations.com). For those who are academically-minded, graduate and postgraduate brewing courses are available at Heriot-Watt University in Edinburgh (www.icbd.hw.ac.uk) and the University of Nottingham (pgstudy.nottingham.ac.uk). Similar courses are available in other countries.

3: Appreciating beer

The tasting experience

Everyone's flavour perceptions are different and ultimately dictate whether they like a beer

The taste of beer is inevitably a personal matter. Everyone's flavour perceptions are different and ultimately dictate whether they like a beer. However, the actual components of the taste of a beer are much more clearly defined. This chapter helps you to identify those components and to work out for yourself what it is that you like or dislike about a beer.

I've discussed how the main flavouring ingredients in beer are malt (and other cereals) and hops, showing as well how the water and the action of the yeast also impact on a beer's taste. Now it's time to look more closely at those ingredients and take a look at the science of tasting, how to identify individual beer flavours and how to record your findings so that your enjoyment of beer is enhanced.

Appearance

The tasting process starts not with the mouth or even the nose, but the eye. It is hard to deny that the appreciation of a beer begins simply by looking at it. If a beer is bright, rich in colour and topped with a good collar of foam – not to mention presented in an attractive glass – the drinker already begins to think favourably about it. Conversely, if the beer is flat, cloudy (perhaps with bits floating in it) and has a feeble, scummy head, first impressions are not great.

The other importance of taking a good look at a beer first is that it can very often tell you what the beer is going to taste like. We've seen that the brewer has a wide variety of malts and other cereals to play with when creating a beer recipe, and we've seen how pale malts produce light-coloured wort and malts that have spent longer in the kiln add shades of darkness – anything from light amber to pitch black. You can therefore bear all this in mind when taking a first look at a beer. If it is yellow or golden in colour, then the chances are that the brewer has used only the very palest, most delicate malts – pale ale malt or lager malt perhaps. This means that the beer is unlikely to have pronounced malt flavours and even less likely to exhibit notes of toffee, caramel, nut, chocolate and coffee that come from the use of darker malts. Alternatively, if the beer has a deep brown colour, for instance, then those darker malts will more than likely be well in evidence in the aroma and taste.

Linked to this use of malts is the use of hops. It makes no sense for a brewer who is hoping to showcase the finer qualities of one or more varieties of hop to create a malt base that is full of intrusive malt flavours. The character of the hops is going to be masked or even obliterated as a result. Hence a brewer wanting to showcase hops tends to use a pale wort, created from pale malts – a blank canvas, if you like, on which to paint hoppy pictures. The opposite of this scenario is when a brewer wants to make a richly malty beer, or one with a deep roasted grain character. Hops in this case play second fiddle, so there's little point in using hops with extravagant flavours. Most stouts, for example, are hopped with solid, bittering strains that are not known for their aromas. Of course, in this anything-goes world of beer in which we live today, it is quite possibly to find beers that defy all the above logic – so-called black IPAs, for example – but the sight test does still generally help you identify what sort of beer you're going to be drinking before it even approaches your nose or lips. Some brewers recognize this in their marketing and point-of-sale material. Chiltern brewery in Buckinghamshire, for example, has a range of pumpclips with an image of the beer being dispensed, so giving customers a chance to see what the beer will actually look like.

Tip

Keeping the bottom of the glass on the table while swirling the contents usually helps prevent the beer from sloshing over the sides.

Aroma

After analysing the appearance of a beer, the next stage involves assessing the aroma. Why should we do this? Well, for a number of reasons, beginning with its actual suitability for consumption. Many people sniff milk, to see if it's gone off, before pouring it on their breakfast cereals. In the same way, most people – albeit inadvertently – sniff their beer and are easily deterred by anything unpleasant that indicates that there's a fault. Obvious warning aromas include vinegar (most common with cask beer that has not been sold quickly enough), farmyard (usually evidence of bacterial infection, but sometimes deliberate) and green apples (symptomatic of a beer that is not fully fermented and not yet ready to serve). A full list of such off aromas and flavours is provided later.

Assuming the beer passes the fit-for-consumption test, the other importance of sniffing the beer is that, like gauging the appearance, it can predict how the beer is going to taste in the mouth. In fact, it is actually the first stage of that tasting process because most of the human taste sensors lie not on the tongue, or elsewhere in the mouth, but in the nose. Even when you are drinking the beer, most of the flavour identification is carried out by the nose. If you doubt this, consider the last time you had a heavy cold and couldn't taste anything. This was very probably because your nose was blocked and those nasal flavour sensors were unable to do their job.

The best way to assess the aroma of a beer is to pour a small quantity into a glass, leaving plenty of room for you to swirl the glass without spilling the beer. For obvious reasons, this is not such an easy procedure to undertake in a pub with a brim-full pint glass but, in the comfort of your own home, you can dictate how much beer you pour into the glass. It helps if you use a glass that tapers inwards at the top, to hold in the aroma, and has a stem you can hold it by, to prevent your hand from warming the glass, but don't get too hung up on glassware at this stage. Take the glass and gently swirl the beer around. The swirling motion agitates the beer and causes carbonation bubbles to break out of solution. These rise to the surface lifting aromas from within the beer to your nose. Don't just take one long sniff; take several short sniffs. Try this a few times, giving your nose a rest for a few seconds in between. Don't be put off if you struggle to find much aroma at first, or if you can't work out what you're actually smelling. With time and experience, everything will slot into place.

Taste and finish

When you finally get around to tasting the beer, don't bolt it. Allow the beer to wash over your tongue so that all the tastebuds and other flavour sensors in the mouth have a chance to do their work and can pick out whatever flavours there may be: sweetness, bitterness, sourness, salt, savoury, malt, hops and more. Don't forget that your nose is also still active at this point, so the longer the beer is in the mouth, the more chance the sensors in the nose have to pick up aromas that rise up through the back of the throat. To help the nose do its work, while the beer is in the mouth, you can suck in a little air that pushes the aromas up the nose, or expel a little air through the nose just after swallowing the beer.

Also while the beer is in the mouth, you have the chance to assess the mouthfeel. This means the texture of the beer, the fullness of body and the sensations experienced on the palate. You might find beers that appear rather thin for the strength, for instance, or ones that are thick and oily. There are also beers that have an astringency that puckers the palate, while others may be grainy or creamy. The level of carbonation will change the way beer feels in the mouth, as will alcohol or spiciness that results in warmth.

The final stage of tasting beer is the one everyone has been waiting for. You swallow it! Unlike in wine tasting, this is an important aspect of the beer-tasting procedure, the reason being that the aftertaste, or finish as it is called, produces different flavours, or intensity of flavours, from those up to now detected in the mouth. In particular, sweetness and malt character tend to fade (sometimes rather quickly) and dryness, bitterness and hop flavours linger or build. This means that a beer that is, say, relatively sweet and fruity to taste may finish bitter, dry and herbal. As this is probably what the brewer intended, it would therefore be quite wrong to spit out the beer and only see part of the picture. Furthermore, the dryness that is often found in the finish is a key aspect of the enjoyment and drinkability of the beer. If a beer ends sweet and cloying, there's probably not much chance of your wanting to drink a lot more of it, whereas a beer with a dry finish leaves you slightly thirsty and desiring another.

The texture of the beer, fullness of body and sensations on the palate are known as mouthfeel

Technicalities

As described above, evaluation of flavour is a joint venture between the nose and the mouth. The nose is a highly sophisticated piece of sensory equipment. In humans, it contains around 10 million receptor cells. Most of these olfactory receptors are located in the lining at the back of the nasal cavity. They are coated in mucus (sorry if this sounds a little unpleasant) and, when chemical molecules in the air dissolve in the mucus, the receptors are stimulated and send messages to the brain accordingly. The signals also pass to other parts of the brain, including those responsible for memory. That is why certain smells bring bouts of nostalgia and also explains why you can associate aromas in beer with aromas you've encountered elsewhere, be they fruits, flowers, biscuits, vinegar or whatever. However, when you have a cold, the mucus is too thick for the receptors to react.

Taste in the mouth is detected primarily on the tongue but also in certain other areas at the back and on the sides. On the tongue, the flavour receptors are called tastebuds. You can't see them but they are housed within bumps that you can see, which are called papillae. Humans have around 10,000 tastebuds plus, to a lesser degree, other sensory organs elsewhere in the mouth. Each responds to different taste sensations, detecting five known components: sweet, salt, sour, bitter and umami (savouriness). It was long thought that these sensations were detected on defined areas of the tongue (for example, sweetness at the front) but that is no longer the scientific analysis. It seems all parts of the tongue cover all sensations, although sourness tends to be detected on the sides towards the back and bitterness strongly at the back – one further reason why it is important to swallow beer during a tasting. It is also now thought that the tongue detects a sixth sensation – fat. However, as there is no fat in beer, that's not relevant here. As with the olfactory sensors in the nose, tastebuds react to chemical molecules in the food or drink and send signals to the brain. The tongue is also responsible for helping to gauge mouthfeel.

Flavours

It is clearly important to understand what the main flavouring components of beer are before embarking on any tasting trials. Various ways have been devised of indicating which flavours can be found and where they come from. One of the most popular is the flavour wheel. This is a circular diagram divided into segments, like a dartboard. Broad flavour characteristics are highlighted in the centre and then these are broken down into more precise flavour notes in segments spanning outwards. Included are off flavours. The idea is to provide the industry with standard language for describing beer, but the principle has been adapted at various times, for example to pinpoint which flavours come from which ingredients or brewing processes. Similar information can be provided in simple table form, as below.

Source	Aroma / flavour / sensation
Pale/lager malt	biscuit, bread, cereal, cracker, grain, honey, malty bedtime drinks, sweetness
Darker malts	bitterness, burnt grain, caramel, chocolate, coffee, cola, leather, liquorice, malt loaf, nut, raisin, roasted grain, smoke, toast, tobacco, toffee
Other cereals	bread, cream, nut, spices
Hops	berries, bitterness, cedar, citrus fruit, earthiness, flowers, grape, grass, herbs, nettle, orchard fruit, pepper, pine, pith, resin, sap, stone fruit, tropical fruit, zest
Fermentation	alcohol, almond, apple, banana, bubblegum, clove, fortified wine, pear drop, tropical fruit, warmth
Sugar	molasses, sweetness
Water	chalk, crispness, dryness, minerals, salt, sulphur, sweetness
(Wood) ageing	acidity, balsamic vinegar, (coconut), oak, sourness, (spirit), (vanilla)

To complicate matters, everyone has their own detection threshold for flavours. Some people can pick up sulphur, for example, at a very low level, while other people may remain blind to it even when present at a high level. Furthermore, some people are naturally expert tasters, as their sensory equipment is very finely attuned. These are the people that major breweries employ on their internal tasting panels. They are discovered through tasting trials and then trained to identify specific flavours and off-flavours. Working individually, but with results collated as a team, these tasters provide valuable information to the brewery. This may be about the brewery's own beers – consistency of flavour, potential problems, etc. – or about rivals' beers – particularly useful in product development when a brewery is trying to replicate the successful attributes of an existing beer. Their role is different from that of the drinker, however. They often just score flavour intensities by numbers and may not be asked for any preferences. They may not even be regular beer drinkers. It is a very cold, analytical process, quite removed from the enjoyment of beer, especially when you factor in all the other elements that impact on a drinker's perception of a beer, everything from environment, climate and company to personal thirst, tiredness and recent food intake. All these factors mean that beer drinking is not the same as beer tasting, although both can be extremely enjoyable in their own way.

Another factor to bear in mind while tasting beer is that hop flavours, malt flavours and other aspects are never precisely isolated. If you added a particular hop flavour to water, then perhaps you'd get a fairly clear impression of what that flavour is all about. However, when that flavour is in a beer, it is competing and contrasting with any number of other flavours – malt, other hops, fermentation – and so is never detected in its purest form. But this integration with other flavours is also a good thing as flavours often work compatibly or combine to greater effect. Adding black pepper to strawberries has been recognized as a means of bringing out richer strawberry flavours and such flavour synergies are always at work within beer, with malts, hops, water and fermentation products all potentially complementing each other. To complicate matters further, the level of carbonation in a beer changes taste perceptions, as does the temperature of the beer.

All the above goes to show that there can never be one definitive taste description of any beer. At best, we can agree on certain key attributes, and that is enough to provide a profile that helps us decide if it's the sort of beer we would like to drink or not (based on past experience of beers with similar profiles), and to help us find other beers with similar profiles to try or to avoid.

Hands on ✋

To understand the flavour of malt, try one of the following. Buy a bottle of a malty alcohol-free drink such as Mighty Malt (available from some supermarkets). There are some hops in this, but they are negligible in the taste, drowned out by malt flavours and added sugar. Smell and taste the rich malt character, reminiscent of bran flakes, a little treacle and multi-grain bread. It's a close comparison to wort before the hops are added. Alternatively, obtain a jar of malt extract (available from health food stores and some supermarkets). This is normally spread on bread or toast but just try a little neat. A further tasting option is malt loaf (without spreading it with butter or margarine). Soreen is the best-known brand. It contain raisins but the chewy, bready body of the loaf is again rich in deep malt flavours.

Unfortunately, it is not so easy to isolate the flavours of hops, as nearly all drinks including hops are based on malt, even non-alcoholic ones. The best thing to try, if you can get your hands on some whole-leaf hops, is to make a hop tea. Put a couple of spoonfuls of leaves into a mug and pour on boiling water. Leave to infuse for a few minutes, strain, allow to cool for a little while and then smell and taste. It won't be very pleasant – rather harsh and bitter – but it will give you an indication of what hops bring to a beer.

Organizing a tasting

As this book endeavours to prove, there is no substitute for methodically tasting beers in order to understand what they are all about. Reading and visiting breweries provide excellent background, but personal experience of a beer is the only way to fully grasp the concept. This makes it sound like a chore but it's really far from that. Formal tasting can be turned into a great social event by inviting friends and colleagues to join you and share opinions, and it can also be good fun on your own.

This book encourages you to try numerous Taste offs!, generally involving three beers that epitomize a given style. To get the most out of these trials, the following guidelines will be of use. The first thing to do is prepare yourself. It's no good attempting a tasting if you've just finished eating a curry. A clean palate is essential if you are to get the most out of the exercise, so that means no food (especially strong-flavoured food) and no smoking immediately before, and no lingering toothpaste. Also, avoid using aftershaves and perfumes, which can totally dominate the atmosphere. Like all food and drink, beer is best appreciated when slightly hungry and thirsty – although an empty stomach is

Tip 💡

When choosing the best place to conduct your tasting, bear in mind that natural light is helpful, so that you can accurately assess the appearance of the beer, and that a kitchen filled with cooking smells is not a good option.

not recommended for drinking (as opposed to tasting) – so leave it a few hours after a meal before starting. Professional tastings often take place in the morning, when palates are fresh and tasters are not tired or full.

Cool the beers to the correct temperature, as outlined in the later chapter on Buying, storing & serving. Don't try to taste too many beers at once. After a while, your palate will become less sharp and it won't be fair to beers later in the tasting. Ideally, taste no more than half a dozen beers at a time, although three or four is probably an optimum number if your intention is to gain a good understanding of each beer. Choose the same glassware for each beer. We'll look later at how the shape of glasses aids or inhibits aroma and flavour assessment, but what is more important in comparing beers is to give them all an equal chance to shine, which means the same glasses. If your interest in beer tasting grows, then you can invest in more appropriate glassware but, for the moment, a large wine glass will do the job. It is very important, however, to ensure the glass is not warm. This not only heats up the beer but also encourages oxidation, which will tarnish the flavour.

It is customary to taste the beers in order of strength, to avoid the bolder beers corrupting the taste of more delicate ones. In a tasting of mixed beer styles, it is also wise to keep dark beers to the end, as strong roasted grain flavours are hard to wash away and will impact on the taste of lighter beers. The same is true of very hoppy beers, such as US IPAs, and these need to be similarly treated.

Pay particular attention to whether the beer is bottle conditioned or not. Such beers contain a natural sediment and sometimes this is very loose, meaning it will enter the glass and spoil the appearance and change the taste of the beer if the bottle is not handled carefully. If you are planning to make more than one pour from the same bottle (very likely in a tasting scenario), then it's advisable to decant the beer into a jug first. This may remove a little of the natural carbonation but it does at least ensure a clean pour into every glass. Note that some beers come with recommendations to be served with the sediment, so check the labels for any such instructions.

Open the bottles carefully, squeezing the cap with a bottle opener to allow the first hiss of carbonation to escape. Then slowly remove the cap and allow the beer to stand for a few seconds to vent off a little more carbonation. Pour gently, allowing the beer to trickle in at an angle, thus helping to keep the foam under control. Some tasters recommend a more aggressive pour, emptying a good slug into the middle of the glass. This may work fine if you simply plan on drinking the beer but it tends to create too much foam and that can block aromas so it's not such a good option when you're looking to make tasting notes.

As you taste the beers, keep a record of your findings. It is useful to devise a simple tasting form covering all the important areas – appearance, aroma, taste/ mouthfeel and finish – along with the date of the tasting. You may wish to make it more detailed by noting carbonation levels, the amount/looseness of any sediment, the best before date or size of the bottle, for example, but keeping it simple, at least to start with, is a good move.

After opening the first bottle, hold back on making a note of the appearance for the moment, in order to appreciate the aroma when the beer is at its most volatile, using the swirl-and-sniff procedure outlined earlier. Don't, however, taste the beer yet. Instead, open the second bottle and do the same as for the first. Then the third. Now go back to the first beer and check the aroma again. You will be surprised by how much it has developed. You will find it easier to pick out various aromas but also will be struck by how the aromas have changed since the first time around. This is a result of more volatile aromas disappearing, the beer warming slightly in the glass and the initial carbonation working off. Again, however, don't taste the beer just yet. It is an unfortunate and unavoidable consequence of tasting one beer that it will have some impact on the next, so at least keep the aroma assessments as pure as possible by refraining from tasting all beers at this point. Continue to appreciate the newly-opened-up aromas of the second and third beers and then return to beer number one for a final aroma test. Be aware, however, that aromas can linger in your nose between beers and you may have to 'reset' your nasal sensors. A simple way of doing this is to sniff the back of your hand a few times to stimulate a different aroma sensation in the nose and brain.

Tip

You can easily create tasting forms on a computer and print them off to save time writing out the headings every time. A sample tasting form has been prepared to accompany this book and can be downloaded, free of charge, from the author's website (www. insidebeer.com).

Use a pen rather than a pencil when writing tasting notes. Pencils have a much more intrusive aroma and may mask some delicate beer characteristics.

Visit

Look for events hosted by breweries and beer writers, especially tutored tastings. These usually take place in pubs, at beer festivals and at regional food and drink showcases. As well as providing lots of background information about each beer – history, style, etc. – the best of these explain clearly how the colours, aromas and flavours have arrived in the glass, analysing the ingredients and brewing processes. Some introduce beer and food pairing. Two regular events in particular are worth noting, with CAMRA specialists hosting tutored tasting sessions. The first is the **Great British Beer Festival** (www.gbbf.org.uk), held at Olympia, London, in August. The second is the **BBC Good Food Show** (www. bbcgoodfoodshowwinter. com), staged at the NEC, Birmingham, in November.

Now you can move on to properly assessing the appearance. It is often useful to hold the glass up to the light, in order to gain a true indication of colour. A beer that appears brown may in fact be ruby when held to the light. However, avoid using artificial lights for this as they are often coloured yellow and will alter the colour of the beer slightly. This process will also highlight any haze in the beer. If it does, this may be intentional – some beers are designed to be served that way – but it may also indicate a problem, such as bacterial infection. Sometimes the haze is just a harmless by-product of cooling the beer, with proteins and other materials binding together at a low temperature. This is known as a chill haze and will disappear as the beer warms.

At last you can now go on to taste the beer, using the procedure mentioned earlier and making sure you also have another good sniff of the aroma as you do so. The key point is to allow the beer time in the mouth, so swirl it around your tongue for several seconds. See what flavours you can now pick up and how they match or differ from the aromas you have already noted. It may be anathema to some but it also pays to spit out the beer at this stage and not swallow. A small bowl is useful here, to avoid trips to the sink. As described earlier, the finish of the beer, after you have swallowed it, brings forth different flavours and these will inevitably influence your next mouthful. By tasting and spitting a few times, you can nail down the taste flavours and then swallow to gauge the finish, allowing around 20 seconds after swallowing to give the finish time to build. After swallowing a few mouthfuls, you should have put together a good profile of the beer and can move on to the next.

In an ideal world, your palate should now be clean and fresh, but of course it's not going to be, having just tasted a beer. To mitigate this, it pays to have plenty of still water at hand. This can be tap water, if the local supply is not too heavily chlorinated, but may have to be bottled mineral water. Rinse out your mouth several times, licking your lips to remove any lingering beer and swallowing some of the water to flush out the finish of the last beer. Some people also like to eat something neutral to remove the taste of the last beer. This can be a plain cracker, a small cube of bread or an unflavoured American-style pretzel. This can certainly help but, if you do eat anything, rinse your mouth with water again before continuing the tasting.

At the end of the tasting, compare your notes. If tasting beers of just one style, see what they have in common and identify the nuances that make each beer different. If you're tasting with others, exchange findings and opinions. Very often, a particular flavour characteristic may not be obvious to you until someone else mentions it and then suddenly you wonder how you missed it. For this reason, if you're tasting alone, it's a good idea to have one or two good

Tasting form

Brewery:

Beer:

Declared style:

Strength:

Date of tasting:

Bottle size:

Bottle conditioned? (yes/no)

Best before date:

Appearance/colour:

Aroma:

Taste/mouthfeel:

Aftertaste:

Score:

General remarks:

Tip

Be wary of online tasting forums. While some of the contributors may be experienced and proficient, many others are less so. The level of misinformation and prejudice that runs through some entries may be confusing and off-putting if you're still new to the concept.

Read on

Melissa Cole, *Let Me Tell You About Beer* (Pavilion, 2011)

Randy Mosher, *Tasting Beer* (Storey Publishing, 2009)

Roger Protz, *The Taste of Beer* (Weidenfeld & Nicolson, 1998)

Gregg Smith, *The Beer Enthusiast's Guide* (Storey Publishing, 1994)

books handy so you can look up the style of beer, learn more about it and compare your tasting notes. You may also like to consult the flavour table on p75. Just reminding yourself to look for various malt components, hop flavours or fermentation by-products will ensure you don't miss anything as you taste. But there is a danger here. If you read somewhere that a certain beer should have a particular flavour, there may be a temptation to exaggerate it in your notes. Always defer to what you actually taste and not what is expected of you.

You may also wish to score the beers in some way, just to provide a quick future reference about your preferences. You can give scores out of perhaps 10 or 100 or maybe award stars or medals – gold, silver, bronze or no medal at all. Obviously, it'll be up to you to decide, based on personal taste, what constitutes a good score or a star/medal threshold. Alternatively, you could just award scores on the basis of quality and adherence to the style guidelines, as they do in many beer competitions, and you could also factor in the drinkability of the beer: it may taste really good but how much of it could you drink? Some beers are very flavoursome but are hard to finish. However, the key thing is not to make the concept of tasting too onerous and administrative. Just enjoy the experience and remember that it is always a learning process.

Technicalities

Regrettably, not all aromas and flavours in beer are good. Sometimes, something has gone wrong between the brewer starting out with the best intentions and the beer arriving in your glass. The table opposite will help you recognize such problems and identify the cause.

Formal training

Exploring and finding out for yourself about beer flavours is a great way to learn about beer but some people may seek a more formal introduction, or may wish to build on their knowledge with some advanced training. A number of organizations now help with this, including CAMRA (www.camra.org.uk), which arranges training as part of its tasting-panel structure that provides the tasting notes seen in the annual *Good Beer Guide*. The training is open to all CAMRA members and is free of charge. Sessions are held in various locations around the UK several times a year.

The Beer Academy (www.beeracademy.co.uk) also offers a number of courses that explore beer tasting and these are held in a number of UK locations. Fees vary according to the duration and scope of the course. Equivalent courses

Off flavours

Aroma/flavour	Common cause*	Technical term
Baby vomit	Bacterial infection	Butyric acid
Butterscotch	Fermentation defect	Diacetyl
Cardboard/wet paper	Oxygen contamination	Oxidation
Cheese	Stale hops/bacterial infection	Isovaleric acid
Cooked vegetables	Slow wort cooling	Dimethyl sulphide (DMS)
Disinfectant	Chlorine contamination	Chlorophenol
Farmyard	Fermentation defect	4-ethyl phenol
Green apple	Fermentation defect	Acetaldehyde
Harsh dryness	Over-sparging	Astringency
Heat	Fermentation defect	Alcohol
Marmite	Yeast breakdown	Autolysis
Metallic	Contact with iron	Metallic
Mouldy	Poorly stored grains	Fungal contamination
Plastic	Chlorine contamination	Chlorophenol
Skunky	Exposure to light	Isopentyl mercaptan
Solvent	Fermentation defect	Ethyl acetate
Sourness	Bacterial infection	Acidity
Soy sauce	Yeast breakdown	Autolysis
Sulphur	Fermentation defect/water	Hydrogen sulphide
Sweat	Fermentation defect	Caprylic acid
Sweetcorn	Slow wort cooling	Dimethyl sulphide (DMS)
Tomatoes	Slow wort cooling	Dimethyl sulphide (DMS)
Vinegar	Bacterial infection	Acidity

*There is often more than one cause of the problem.

Note that not all these flavours are always unwanted. Some beer styles are deliberately sour, for example, and others can acceptably feature a little DMS or diacetyl.

are offered in the US and Canada by the Cicerone Certification Program (cicerone.org) and some of these are now available in Europe.

Training can also be done at home, using kits provided by companies such as FlavorActiV (www.flavoractiv.com). This Oxfordshire-based business works with breweries all over the world, providing training and sensory analysis of their products, but it also sells kits that can be use for self-teaching. These include capsules of flavourings that, when used to spike a basic beer, exhibit off flavours. In the US the Siebel Institute of Technology (www.siebelinstitute.com), based in Chicago, offers a similar service as, again, does the Cicerone Certification Program.

Hands on ✋

A number of companies produce flavour kits to help you identify off flavours in a beer. But there are some off flavours you can learn to spot without this extra help. These include the vegetal characteristics of what is known as lightstrike, and the paper flavours of oxidation.

For the first, look for a golden beer that is sold in green glass. Buy two bottles. Keep one in a dark space and leave the other exposed to either sunlight or artificial light. You can even speed this up by leaving the bottle on a window sill. After a couple of weeks, flip the cap off each bottle and sniff them immediately. You will find that the exposed bottle has a markedly more unpleasant aroma,

a cabbage-like vegetal note that is known to American drinkers as skunk (drinkers in other parts of the world are not as familiar with the odour sprayed by a skunk). This is the effect of lightstrike. It's tempting to go for clear glass bottles for this experiment, but there are two drawbacks to this. Firstly, the bottles may have already suffered from light contamination by the time you buy them and, secondly, some beers sold in clear glass (mostly international lager brands) are brewed with hops that have been modified so that they do not react in the same way. Green glass is therefore more reliable for this experiment, but more time needs to be allowed.

To learn about oxidation, take two identical beers. Make sure they are pasteurized – or at least filtered – beers and not bottle conditioned, as the yeast still working in the beer will render this experiment less effective. With a bottle opener, gently loosen the cap of one of the bottles. Do not remove the cap entirely, just make a tiny gap so that air is able to enter the bottle. Try not to allow too much carbonation to escape and then, to help things along, blow some air underneath the cap. Leave both beers in your beer store for a couple of weeks and then taste. The beer that has been open to the air will have developed a stale taste that is often described as cardboard or papery. This is the effect of oxidation.

TASTE OFF!

Crystal malt

Once you are comfortable with identifying general beer flavours, you can then progress to looking more closely at individual aspects of those flavours and the causes of them. For example, you may wish to understand more about the contribution of crystal malt. Here are three beers that exemplify (or not) the character of crystal malt; the first two have plenty, the last has none. Remember that this type of malt has been produced by stewing the grains in high humidity in the kiln. This has converted the starch into sugar. This sugar has then been caramelized by ramping up the heat. You would expect, therefore, to find variations on a theme of caramel, toffee and burnt sugar notes in the beer, as well as an amber-brown colouring.

Ridgeway Ivanhoe

Showing crystal malt character throughout, this amber-coloured ale has a pleasant nuttiness beneath its fragrant floral, peachy hop notes.

Wadworth Old Timer

Although there is some orange and raisin fruitiness in this copper-coloured beer, it doesn't obscure the caramel notes of the crystal malt that run from aroma to finish.

Wye Valley HPA

This is the control example, the beer to compare against, as the pale straw colour and the complete absence of caramel or toffee flavours reveals. Zesty lemon and floral notes feature instead.

Buying, storing & serving

When it comes to buying, storing and serving beer there are a few rules that should be followed to guarantee the maximum enjoyment. Of course, there are easy pleasures to be had by simply filling a supermarket basket with bottles and pouring them into a tumbler when you get home but, for full appreciation, it pays to be a little more fastidious.

The first thing to consider is where you buy your beer. Supermarkets today certainly have a far greater choice than they have traditionally offered, but look closely and you'll find that only a small percentage of the beers they stock are truly great. There are many perfectly acceptable beers on the shelves but not a lot that is really special. Add to that the fact that supermarkets are brightly lit, which leads to the danger of lightstrike, mentioned earlier, especially on beers packaged in clear or green glass, and that they operate mostly at room temperature, and you can see that the supermarket aisle is not really the best place to store beer, however tempting the special offers may be.

A better option is the specialist beer retailer, where you are likely to find a far wider variety and many more beers that are touched by greatness. This is because such shops have to offer something different from the supermarket around the corner, which will always beat them on price. The range is more focused and more carefully chosen. The owners are generally enthusiasts themselves, whereas supermarket beer buyers (although some are now very knowledgeable) tend to be career retail executives whose previous role might have involved buying soap powder and whose next promotion will take them to biscuits. There is also more of an interactive element in independent shops. Customers and proprietors talk openly about the beers on the shelves, comparing experiences, making suggestions. This results in the shop tailoring its offering towards beers that are truly appreciated by its clientele, taking on board not just bare sales statistics but also useful feedback.

Another good option is mail order. Most of the successful internet retailers are well clued up about their products. Factoring in shipping can make their offering a bit more expensive but this is offset in some cases by the sheer number of beers to choose from, as they operate out of warehouses rather than limited shop premises. This may also have the added benefit of keeping beer cooler and out of the damaging presence of light.

When it comes to actually buying the beer, it makes sense to play the game to your advantage. If you're in a shop, you can spot the best before dates on each bottle and so check whether the stock is old (if the shop is poorly managed, dust on the bottles will also be a giveaway). Most beer, let's remember, is designed to be drunk fresh, and the further away the best before date is, the greater the likelihood that the beer has been bottled fairly recently. There are instances where the best before date does not matter: strong beers can improve with age but, even in such circumstances, you may wish to buy the beer as young as possible and age it in an environment where you can fully control how the beer is going to be kept.

The other little trick that can sometimes help is to check out the layout of the shop and see where the sun falls during certain times of the day. The best position for a beer shop is with its back to the south (in the northern hemisphere), as this means there is little or no direct sunlight beaming through the windows. Most retailers are fully aware of this problem and organize their displays accordingly, but it can sometimes happen that shelves are badly positioned so it's more likely that the best preserved beer will be found in another corner of the shop. Even here you can try to eliminate any light intrusion by selecting a bottle from the back of the shelf, rather than the one that is fronting the display, as there is more chance it will not be caught in the glare of a neon tube or a spotlight. Needless to say, any bottle that has been used in a window display should not be considered. Finally, always feel the temperature of bottles on the shelf. Warm bottles do not bode well. In the US, attention to temperature is precise, with many liquor stores having walk-in coolers.

storing

Once you've brought your bottles home, unless you plan to drink them all very soon, you'll need to observe the basic principles of good shopkeeping to ensure the beer stays in good condition. This means keeping the bottles in a consistently cool, dark place (ideally approximately 10–14°C/50–57°F). If the beers are bottle conditioned, you should also keep them upright, to allow the sediment to settle at the bottom. Some people argue that beers with a cork should be laid down, to enable the beer to keep the cork moist. If the cork dries out, then oxygen may creep into the bottle and speed up the staling process. If you do lay down bottles, remember to return them to the vertical a few days before you plan to open them, to allow the sediment to settle back to the bottom. However, be aware that if the beer has been horizontal for a long period of time, yeast may have settled along the side of the bottle and may not drop to the bottom, which may result in a hazy beer as you pour.

To serve beer at its best, you need to observe the optimum temperature for the style. Personal preferences may lead you to always choose to drink beer at room temperature or ice-cold from the fridge. If that's what you enjoy, that's all that matters. However, if you really want to appreciate what the brewer has intended then follow the guidelines in the following chart.

Recommended serving temperatures

Temperature	Styles
Cold: 5–8°C (41–46°F)	Altbiers, bocks, dark lagers, fruit lambics, gose, gueuze, helles, kölsch, pale lagers, rauchbier, witbiers, weizens
Cool: 10°C (50°F)	Flemish reds, golden ales, oud bruins, saisons, summer ales
12°C (54°F)	Bières de garde, bitters, brown ales, IPAs, milds, old ales, pale ales, porters, stouts, strong ales, Trappist and abbey beers
Fresh: 14°C (57°F)	Barley wines, imperial stouts, wood-aged beers

Achieving exact serving temperatures can be difficult in a domestic environment. Very few people have dedicated beer cellars or beer fridges, where the temperature can be set precisely at a certain point. Most of us have to make do with the kitchen fridge, where the focus, understandably, is on the right temperature to keep meat and dairy products at the correct temperature (usually between 0º and 5ºC/32º and 41ºF). To work around this, you may have to adjust the time you leave beer in the fridge. Digital thermometers are available so that you can test how cold the beer is after spending time in the fridge. By keeping records, you can then learn how long the appropriate cooling time should be to achieve a required temperature. For most of us, however, that's just too fiddly, and we're happy to work to three basic temperature parameters, which I call cold, cool and fresh.

The terms largely speak for themselves. Cold means beer that has been very well refrigerated, cool means comfortably below room temperature (although some beers need to be slightly cooler than others – see table opposite), and fresh is just refreshing, around 14ºC (57ºF). It's tempting to describe the last as ambient temperature but that doesn't help, as ambient temperature can vary dramatically. Basically, you just want to take the edge off so the beer is not tepid and yet not so chilled that you start to mask the flavours.

Technicalities

As mentioned, some beers actually benefit from longer time in the bottle. These tend to be beers that are strong and full bodied. The alcohol acts as a preservative and the richness of the beer allows plenty of scope for subtle flavour shifts to take place over time. A generous supply of hops, with their own natural preservative quality, also helps.

Flavours do change through ageing. With Belgian Trappist beers, for instance, or beers such as vintage ales, the results can be spectacular, but not all the flavour changes in aged beers are beneficial and the beers may not taste as good as when they were young. Generally, hop flavour subsides, sugars are eaten away – making the beer dry and more carbonated – and oxidation can also play a hand, bringing fortified wine notes. The yeast may also break down over time, adding a rubbery or Marmite character to the taste. So it's always a bit of a gamble. The result may be superb, so it is definitely worth experimenting, but it may also be disappointing. Bear in mind, too, that beers may improve or decline from month to month. It's been noted that, because of the chemistry and biology involved in the ageing process, some beers ride a wave of quality, peaking in brilliance at various points in the cycle, falling into troughs where they are less impressive and then picking up again a few months further on.

Another aspect of the maturation process is that beers tend to become slightly darker. This is a result of something called the Maillard reaction, which occurs between sugars and proteins, mainly during boiling but also over time in the bottle.

For ageing, bottle-conditioned beers around 5% ABV and above tend to work best. There's plenty of alcohol to battle any bacteria that may spoil the flavour and enough body so that the beer does not become thin as the yeast continues its work in the bottle. Additionally, the yeast scavenges any oxygen that remains in the beer, helping to prevent premature staling. These beers can be trusted to deliver an excellent taste experience for several months, if not longer. Sour beers are even more resilient but, even if bottle conditioned, more delicate and low-alcohol beers really do have to be consumed young because they don't contain much alcohol or residual sugar. The yeast will quickly eat through the sweetness and leave the beer dry and very gassy. Below is a very rough guide to optimum drinking times for bottle-conditioned beers, but results vary from brewery to brewery (for filtered beers, just stick to the best before dates).

Of course, it's not always easy for customers to work out how old a beer is when they're buying it, and therefore how long to keep it. As an aid for consumers, typical best before date periods used by each brewery are provided in CAMRA's *Good Bottled Beer Guide* so that customers know roughly how old the beer is at the point of sale.

Optimum drinking times

Strength	Drink within
Up to 4.5%	6 months (less for the weakest beers)
4.6–6%	1 year (more for the strongest beers)
6.1%+	18 months–2 years (several years for the strongest beers)

TASTE OFF!

Ageing

To examine the effect of ageing beers, sample three different versions of an annually dated beer such as Fuller's Vintage Ale or Lees Harvest Ale, including the very youngest one available. Such beers not being cheap, it's an expensive exercise, so invite some friends. You don't want to waste these little treats!

Fuller's Vintage Ale 2014

Clean and fresh-tasting, this amber beer has bright aromas and flavours of oranges, plums and floral notes. There's a gentle warmth and it's mostly sweet, with plenty of sugary elements, turning slowly bitter in the finish where oranges linger and there's a modest hop character.

Fuller's Vintage Ale 2009

This is notably less fresh-tasting than the younger beer, but there is still an orange fruitiness, along with dried vine fruits and a creamy maltiness that continues into the dry, smoothly-bitter finish. After six years in the bottle, its flavours are less vibrant than when young but maturity brings a mellowness and richness.

Fuller's Vintage Ale 2004

Ageing has clearly darkened this beer, compared with the other two, giving a ruby blush to the dark amber. When this was tasted young, I noted tangerines and hints of marzipan, rounded off by a hoppy and mostly bitter finish. Eleven years on, the flavours have melded into butter toffee and raisins, with a strange floral note. Remarkably drinkable for its age but a notch down from the first two. Perhaps it will bounce back over a further period of time.

Glassware

Having achieved the correct (or approximately correct) temperature for your beer, you need to ensure that it is served in suitable glassware. You can simply enjoy a beer from a straight pint glass or a plain tumbler but there is so much more to be gained by choosing the correct drinking vessel.

The first pleasure comes from the visual attraction of a beer in an elegant glass. Branded glasses are increasingly common, particularly for Belgian beers. Some brewers will tell you that it is important to always use the right branded glass, as it has been designed to bring out the best qualities of the beer. There may be some truth in this, although the main reason most insist on branded glassware, especially in pubs and bars, is for marketing. It puts the beer name on show to other drinkers. Admittedly, it does feel a little odd to serve, for example, an Orval in a Rochefort glass, but as the shape of the glasses is similar, it is largely an aesthetic thing rather than a practical issue.

Beyond simple visual appeal, the shape of the vessel and the thickness of the glass are physical elements that actually do dictate how a beer will smell and taste, so treat yourself to some quality beer glasses and take your beer appreciation to a new level. As discussed earlier, you will need some decent glasses for analytical tasting. Good wine glasses will do but proper beer-tasting glasses will help you raise your game. However, even for the simple pleasure of drinking, it is worth investing in a small selection of glasses that will bring out the best of most styles of beer. Specialist beer shops and online retailers often sell these. They are usually branded but that's not important.

For pilsner a tall narrow glass is appropriate, preferably one that tapers outwards as, by creating a sort of wedge effect, it supports the foam at the top. As bitterness usually migrates into the foam, this is an important feature, giving that initial hoppy hit on tasting. For other lagers, both pale and dark, a similarly tall, but straighter, glass works well.

For an ale such as mild or bitter, don't be pressured into thinking it has to be a pint glass. A smaller glass with a stem, a round bottom and a curved-in top (often called a tulip) presents the beer far more attractively than a big vessel and also helps retain the aroma. Some varieties of tulip curve back out again at the very top to support any appropriate foam. There are some pint glasses that are quite attractive but the straight sleeve and the pub standard nonic (the one with the bulge just below the top) are possibly the least favourable glasses for the enjoyment of ale, both aesthetically and sensorially. It's hardly a wonder that pub drinkers are somewhat sceptical of beer tasting when the glasses they use are next to useless in maximizing the aromas and flavours of a beer. If you are

Recommended glassware

Chalice or
goblet

Pilsner glass

Weizen glass

Stemmed tulip

concerned about stopping and starting the pour of a bottle-conditioned beer in a pint, or larger, bottle, in case it disturbs the sediment, just decant the beer into a jug first, with one slow pour, keeping an eye on the bottle, as usual, for signs of the sediment approaching the neck. For stronger beers, both ales and lagers, a tulip will again do the business, but a goblet or chalice, as used by many Belgian breweries, certainly gives a lift to Trappist and abbey beers, echoing in its design the holy origins of the beer.

Finally, there is definitely one further glass that you should seek to acquire and that is for weizens. This type of beer is characterized by lively carbonation and so the German weizen glass resembles a tall vase with a bulbous top that allows for a big, fluffy head to develop.

Having bought, stored and cooled your beer, and then selected a suitable glass, don't go ruining your hard work by not washing the glass properly. If the glass is dirty or dusty, it will cause carbon dioxide to break out in small bubbles which cling to the side of the glass. Dishwashers are a mixed blessing. They may

TASTE OFF!

Glassware

To understand how important glassware is to beer appreciation, take one beer and pour equal quantities into a straight half-pint glass and a good wine glass that tapers in towards the top. Without swirling the beers in the glasses (which would even things up), compare the aromas. It is remarkable how much more aroma the wine glass delivers. You can also try drinking the same beer out of a chunky half-pint mug and a delicate wine glass to see how the glass itself can be a barrier to flavour. With a thick glass, your mouth shapes differently when drinking, directing beer further back on the tongue, blocking some immediate work by your tastebuds and giving a duller taste sensation. Also, although glass has a neutral taste, that big chunk of material is intrusive, deflecting attention from the beer. The finer wine glass places the beer right at the front of the mouth, allowing all taste receptors to get in on the act.

save effort but the fierceness of the washing procedure can scratch glassware, affecting how the beer pours and also leaving the glass itself opaque. Unless you have access to professional glassware detergent, dishwashers also may leave an invisible film that will kill the head on a beer. That said, as long the glasses are thoroughly rinsed after removal from the dishwasher, for most occasions the cleaning is adequate. Hand-washing is a better option, but only for the fastidious or to take particular care of cherished glassware. Glasses should be washed with a low-sud detergent but not employing cloths or brushes used for other washing up, so that no food particles are passed on to the glass. They should then be thoroughly rinsed and left to air dry, upside down on a corrugated draining board. Do not dry them with a cloth, as you may leave traces of cotton or other fabric on the inside of the glass.

Technicalities

The Boston Beer Company in the US takes glassware very seriously, so much so that it has designed a specific glass to bring the best out of its Samuel Adams Boston Lager. The glass has a peculiar shape, curving in and out. The bottom of the glass is narrow, making it easier to hold and minimizing heat transfer from your hand, and the base is etched by laser to create a friction point that will constantly cause carbon dioxide to break out of suspension, generating more bubbles. The bulbous parts of the glass trap aromas and the outfacing thin lip delivers the beer comfortably onto the palate.

This may seem to be going to extraordinary lengths to make a point but it does underline the basic principle that the choice of glassware is important to the enjoyment of beer. So, without going to the extremes suggested by Boston Beer, what should we be looking for in a beer-friendly glass?

First of all, it has to be clear, so that you can fully appreciate the appearance of the beer. Next you should be looking at heat transfer and how to minimize this. Glasses with handles, of course, work well from this point of view but they are not particularly popular among the beer-drinking community, especially if the glass is too thick. A stemmed glass is a more elegant and better option as you can pick up the glass without your hands getting anywhere near the contents. Sometimes you want the opposite effect, however, and you might prefer a stemmed glass with a rounded bottom. Barley wines and imperial stouts can become more complex and interesting as they slowly warm in the glass, so your hand can slip up the stem to the bottom of the glass and gradually raise the temperature. The rounded bottom also helps you to swirl the beer to tease out the aromas, while a top that tapers inward holds aromas in the glass for your appreciation.

You will note that all the glasses previously suggested for various styles of beer are stemmed, except the weizen glass, which, like the Boston Beer glass, has a thinner bottom to mitigate heat transfer from the hand.

Thick glass is not ideal for most situations, as you end up almost chewing on the glass with every sip, but it can have its benefits. One reason why beer is served in heavy one-litre mugs in German beer halls and biergartens is that the thickness of the glass helps keep the beer cold.

Pouring

Even if you have a clean glass, it pays to wet it first before pouring your beer. European bars do this as a matter of course as it washes away dust and breaks the surface tension, helping to keep carbonation under control. Wetting the glass can help cool it, too. Beer should never be served into a warm glass – a common failing in the pub trade – as it immediately changes the temperature of the beer. A good idea is to fill the glass with cold water and leave it to stand for a minute or so. This chills the glass nicely. Don't be tempted to follow the discredited American practice of frosting glasses in the freezer. This affects the temperature of the contents as much as warm glasses, and can introduce ice to your beer.

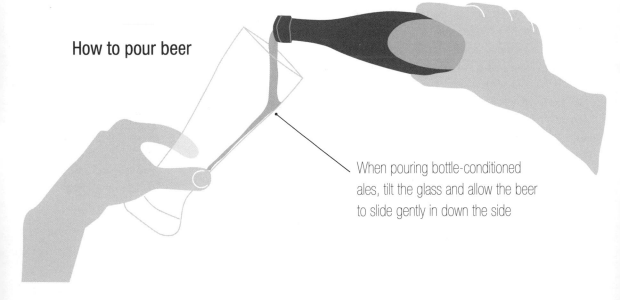

How to pour beer

When pouring bottle-conditioned ales, tilt the glass and allow the beer to slide gently in down the side

The technique of pouring varies according to the style of beer you're drinking, the glassware you've chosen and the appearance you desire. It's been traditional among ale drinkers to do a slow pour, tilting the glass and allowing the beer to gently slide in down the side, then gradually straightening the glass so that a head develops on the top. This is entirely appropriate for many bottle-conditioned beers, where you want to keep the sediment in the bottle, but other forms of beer may be poured differently. In Belgium, for example, experienced waiters know how to serve many strong beers by pouring straight into the middle of the glass and allowing the carbonation to instantly build a head that rises with the beer to the top, just managing to avoid an overspill. It's not an easy method to replicate. Only with practice do you master the flourish that delivers the perfect pour without too much foam. Some people recommend the same approach for all beers, suggesting that it removes excess carbonation from the beer, leaving it less gassy to drink, but this may lead to a bit of stopping and starting in order to fill the glass, and that may not work with bottle-conditioned beers unless they have been previously decanted.

With regard to style of beer, just remember that lagers and weizens are traditionally served with a good head of foam (a couple of inches or more) – normally generated by their naturally high carbonation and important to the texture of the beer and the aromatics of the first sip – so you need to adjust your pouring speed and angles to achieve this.

Read on

Patrick Dawson, *Vintage Beer* (Storey Publishing, 2014)

Jeff Evans, *Good Bottled Beer Guide* (CAMRA Books, 2013)

4: Beer styles

· ·

A family of beers

In 1977, Michael Jackson's *World Guide to Beer* proved to be a ground-breaking publication. It not only took the subject of beer to a new audience, placing it in a gourmet context, it also developed the idea of writing about beer by style. Working country by country, the book presented a taxonomy of beer that made it simple to understand how one style followed on from another and how to identify styles that had elements in common, be they fermentation techniques or ingredients.

Ever since that publication, the world of beer writing has largely worked to Michael's template. With a few notable exceptions, beer books have arranged their contents by beer style. It has been an eminently sensible approach and particularly useful as the beer world has reawakened, casting aside the straitjackets of pilsner-clone lager and brown bitters to rediscover the glories of beers that have long been forgotten, be they authentic IPAs, historic porters or imperial stouts.

As time has progressed, sections of these books have begun to fill out, as breweries have become more adventurous and retailers grown less influenced by big-brand advertising. Also, brewers have taken on a new mantle. From archaeologists, they have turned into inventors. Liberated by the encouragement of the market and facilitated by the development of exotic new hop varieties and the availability of exciting yeast strains, they have started to create beers that no longer fit into the snug glove of a traditional beer style. That's where we are today. We live in a world that is graced by such exotica as black IPAs, dark saisons and wheat wines. Some beers simply defy description. They are what they are: a fusion of historic inspiration and a fertile imagination.

All this begs the questions: 'Are beer styles important any longer?' and 'Should a book such as this be based, still, on beer styles?'. My answer to both is 'Yes'. From a writer's perspective, styles provide a logical, easy-to-follow context in which to structure information about beer. Also, from a brewer's or drinker's point of view, styles, I would say, remain valid. While hard-and-fast rules and regulations clearly don't matter so much these days – unless you're judging in a competition that adheres to such minutiae – there is no doubt that every beer has its roots in one style or another. The black IPA clearly began as an adaptation of a traditional IPA; the dark saison was an attempt to add contrast to the accepted saison style; and the wheat wine simply took barley wine and changed the cereal. Even the more off-the-wall creations that you will stumble across can be traced back to a foundation of some sort in a beer style. It makes sense, therefore, to continue to structure beer education on the style model. Michael Jackson's ahead-of-its-time wisdom remains a benchmark we should still follow.

Beer in print

In Michael's footsteps, the research that has been undertaken into beer styles by historians and brewers has been remarkable. This section of the book draws on this, providing the basic details of what they have unearthed, adding a degree of advanced technical data and then pointing you in the direction of tastings, visits and further reading to take your understanding to a deeper level. Included here are references to various volumes in the Brewers Publications Classic Beer Style series (www.brewerspublications.com). These books are mostly aimed at brewers, and can be rather technical and scientific. That said, they also have good historical sections and provide an excellent insight into the sort of details brewers consider when creating beers.

As well as the books mentioned for each style, there are some notable over-arching works that really should be on your reading list if you intend to fully get to grips with the subject. The first is Martyn Cornell's *Amber, Gold & Black* (The History Press, www.thehistorypress.co.uk), a detailed account of the great beer styles of Britain. Scrupulously researched, it traces the story of 16 different types of beer, from bitter to lager (yes, really), via all the expected styles and even some unexpected, including honey beer and heather ale. The second is Ronald Pattinson's series of self-published books, each covering one style of beer (barclayperkins.blogspot.co.uk). These incredibly detailed works are the result of Ron's passion for digging around in old brewing ledgers. If you want to know exactly how a stout was brewed in London in the 18th century, or a pale ale in Burton in the 19th century, Ron can tell you, down to the last few grains of malt.

For a perspective on the way creative brewers work, you should also refer to the wonderfully clear, online style guide presented by the Brewers Association in the US (www.craftbeer.com/styles). The BA has identified around 80 precise, modern-day beer styles and uses these as a basis for its competitive judging events. There is also more about styles on the CAMRA website: www.camra.org. uk/different-styles.

Discover for yourself

However, reading is one thing. As you work through each style section, there will be no substitute for sipping along with the words. For each style there is at least one Taste off! suggested. This allows you to easily compare and contrast beers that may be variations of that style, or belong to related styles. Instead of being told what the similarities or differences are, you can judge for yourself.

The aim when selecting the beers to Taste off! has been two-fold. Firstly, the beers need to succinctly illustrate the points in question; secondly, they also need to be reasonably easy to get hold of (in some instances, a bit of online research may be required to track down the suggested beer, but most should be obtainable from a well-stocked specialist beer shop and many can be even found in supermarkets). What this means is that the beers are not necessarily presented here as the finest exponents of the style (although some, in my mind, certainly are) but, more practically, as convenient good examples. Bear in mind that, if you are unable to find a required beer, you can simply substitute another example of the style. It is the process of tasting the style, not the precise beer, that is important.

Finally, you don't have to sample the three suggested beers at the same time – maybe opening three bottles just for yourself is a bit too much and, quite rightly, you don't want to pour any away. It's certainly better if you do taste them simultaneously, because the comparison is clearly sharper but, as long as you keep detailed notes, you can always draw conclusions later. Alternatively, share the load, and the cost, by inviting one or two friends to join you.

Pale ales & bitters

Is there a difference between pale ale and bitter? Some brewers and historians argue that there is, but perhaps any difference that exists between the two is simply a matter of packaging. Historically pale ale, it seems, was simply a bottled version of bitter.

The origins of pale ale/bitter date back to the mid-19th century, when British brewers started to produce draught beers that were paler and more heavily hopped than mild and porter, the two styles which, to that point, had dominated brewers' domestic output. These pale beers were weaker versions of the strong, pale, hoppy beers that were being shipped successfully to India, and became known over time as India pale ale (see India pale ales). While it is possible that brewers coined the term 'pale ale' to reflect the fact that the new style was lighter in colour than other beers – thanks to the Industrial Revolution advances that allowed maltsters to dry grains more gently, resulting in new pale-coloured malts – it is less likely that they also came up with the term 'bitter'. That was probably just the response of the drinking public, who – in the absence of pumpclips or other point-of-sale materials, and using their tastebuds – simply latched on to the word as a way of stressing to the barman which of the common beer styles they wanted. In this way, two names for the same beer style came into use. Pale ale became the brewers' preference, marked on casks and bottles, while bitter was what the punters called it.

Over time stronger versions of bitter, with more body from additional malt, and a correspondingly greater input from the hops for balance, became known as best bitters. Until the 1980s it was common to see many British brewers still labelling their beers as simply Bitter and Best Bitter with scant regard for eye-catching, imaginative names. As a rough guideline, bitters range in strength from around 3.4% to 3.9% ABV, with best bitters running from 4% up to around 4.6% or a little above.

For most of the last few decades, the term pale ale took a back seat to bitter, but it is now fully back in everyday parlance, not least because of the influence of American craft brewers who have made the style one of their trademarks. The American pale ale is slightly stronger than the British best bitter, and its other defining feature is the generous hop contribution, with abundant citrus fruit, pine and floral notes coming from American hops.

There is a further extension of the pale ale family that has developed in Belgium. Unlike the US take on the style, the Belgian pale ale has a less obvious hop presence, with more emphasis placed on the subtle perfumed, fruit-and-

For most of the last few decades, the term pale ale took a back seat to bitter, but it is now fully back in everyday parlance

Read on

Terry Foster, *Pale Ale: History, Brewing, Techniques, Recipes* (Brewers Publications, 1999)

Insight

A derivation of the US pale ale is the US amber ale. While fruity American hops still add the dressing, the malt grist includes more crystal or darker malts, to give a deeper colour and a more pronounced caramel/nut flavour. Some versions may be described as red ales. Examples include Anderson Valley Boont Amber Ale and Deschutes Cinder Cone Red Ale.

spice notes created by the chosen yeast. Strength is, again, a touch higher than in a British best bitter.

Technicalities

While, of course, each beer is different and all brewers have their secrets, the basic recipe for a British-style bitter starts with a grist comprising around 85–90% pale ale malt and 5–10% crystal malt. There may be a little wheat (torrefied or wheat malt) or flaked maize, too, to help with head retention, and perhaps some brewing sugar. Historically pale ale, it has been argued, was slightly different from bitter, with crystal malt omitted, but there are plenty of beers described as pale ales today that do include crystal malt. Bitters and pale ales being British in origin, the hops traditionally would have been English, probably similar to the Fuggle, Challenger and Target hops that are commonly used for bitterness today, and to the Golding hops long favoured for aroma. The brewing process is straightforward, with a standard hour-or-so boil and warm fermentation with an ale yeast. Cask-conditioning is the standard for such beers, bringing out the full flavours and all the subtleties of this quaffable beer style.

The American pale ale is similarly built on pale malt with a small quantity of crystal malt but is a more strident beer – a touch stronger (somewhere in the 4.5–6% ABV region) and never afraid to let its hops do the talking. Some US brewers import British malts and then lace them with their own pungent hop varieties, such as Centennial, Cascade and Simcoe. The model has been adapted elsewhere into a sort of New World pale ale style, with brewers in the antipodes offering their own take, influenced by floral, fruity New Zealand and Australian hops. In Belgium bitterness in pale ales is moderate, thanks to the delicate use of English hops or their equally reserved continental equivalents. Replacing crystal malt may be European speciality malts such as Vienna or Munich. The approximate strength of a Belgian pale ale is 5–5.5% ABV but the beer is generally served in smaller measures than the pint associated with British bitter.

TASTE OFF!

Pale ales & bitters

Marston's Pedigree

Pedigree nicely sums up the contribution Burton upon Trent has made to world brewing culture. Sometimes labelled pale ale, at other times marked as a bitter, this easily found but often-overlooked beer exhibits all the virtues of the style – a firm underpinning of bready, barley-sugar malt, leading to a bittersweet taste once the herbal, almost liquorice-like hops have done their work, with hints of apple from the distinctive Marston's yeast and a slight saltiness in the dry, bitter finish.

Sierra Nevada Pale Ale

This may be the benchmark American pale ale but it is by no means the most hoppy. That said, zesty bitter orange notes from the hops characterize the aroma, with more of the same, along with some pine, on top of faint caramel in the mostly bitter taste. Orange peel and pith feature in the dry, tangy, bitter finish. The contrast with the traditional British pale ale is obvious.

De Koninck

The archetypal Belgian pale ale, from Antwerp. Despite being pasteurized for the bottle, the main characteristics of the style are evident. It's just on the bitter side, with hints of caramel, some apple and over-ripe fruit, and the perfumed presence of esters. There's an almost aniseed note in the dry, bitter, herbal-spicy finish.

If you want to try more…

… try these other examples:

British Style: Adnams Bitter, Batemans XXXB, Black Sheep Ale, Fuller's Chiswick Bitter, Harveys Sussex Best Bitter, Hook Norton Old Hooky, Taylor Landlord **American/New World Style:** Anchor Liberty Ale, Flying Dog Doggie Style, Goose Island Honker's Ale, Little Creatures Pale Ale, Thornbridge Kipling **Belgian Style:** De Ryck Special, Palm Speciale, Slaghmuylder Witkap-Pater Special

… you may also like:

brown ale, dunkel, golden ale, India pale ale, strong ale, Vienna

Visit

For a fresh pale ale experience, drink Draught Bass in the **Cooper's Tavern** (www.cooperstavern.co.uk), once the brewery's tap, in Burton upon Trent. Take a tour of the **Sierra Nevada brewery** (www.sierranevada.com) in Chico, California, and discover the roots of the US pale ale style. Savour the Belgian pale ale at its freshest by ordering a bolleke (a local name for a stemmed goblet) of De Koninck in the **Café de Pelgrim** (www.brasseriedepelgrim.be), opposite the brewery in Antwerp, now reopened after a period of closure.

Golden ales

It is a common misconception that golden ales are a recent invention. The truth is that very pale-coloured beers have been in production since the days when maltsters discovered how to create pale-coloured malt. Historians have unearthed references in archives that point to golden ales appearing as early as the 1840s, or even before. There is no question, however, that golden ales have never been as popular as they are today.

For most of the 20th century, golden ales, or blond beers to give them another widely used name, were notable by their absence as British drinkers showed a distinct preference for dark milds and brown bitters. There were exceptions, such as the popular Boddingtons and Stones Bitters in the North of England, but it wasn't until the mid-1980s when the Golden Hill brewery (now known as Exmoor Ales) in Somerset came up with a bright yellow beer called Exmoor Gold, that much excitement was generated around the style. Leaving crystal malt out of the recipe, Exmoor created a beer that looked just like a pint of lager, the heavily advertised product whose sales were rocketing. It seemed like a good plan. If some lager drinkers could be won over (or won back) to the cask ale fold, it would not do any harm. Exmoor Gold immediately turned heads and was followed soon after by Summer Lightning from Hop Back brewery in Wiltshire.

It was the success of this particular beer, in winning the Best New Brewery Beer award at CAMRA's Champion Beer of Britain contest in 1989, that really set brewers thinking. Golden ales began to arrive all over the country. Being pale in colour, these beers – many described as 'summer ales' – were also excellent vehicles for showcasing hops, particularly the newly popular, citrus- and floral-accented hops arriving from the US. Since 2000, golden ale has been the most successful of beer styles in the UK, with so many now produced that a separate category has been set up to judge them at CAMRA's annual awards.

The hallmarks of a British-style golden ale are a modest alcohol level (around 3.5–5% ABV), a very pale colour, a sweetish palate and a delicate hop character based on British or European (lager) hops. Similar beers in the US also have a relatively modest hop profile, contrasting with the hop-forward American pale ale style, but a more robust American style of golden ale has been developed in the UK with brewers packing their palest beers with pungent American hops. There's also a third kind of golden ale that belongs to a different tradition. This comes from Belgium, where beers tend to be stronger than in the UK. Golden ales there are known as blonds. They kick off at around 6% ABV and can rise to

Golden ales have never been as popular as they are today

Visit

For an understanding of the influential Belgian strong golden ale, Duvel, book a tour of the **Duvel Moortgat brewery** (www.duvel.com) at Breendonk, between Brussels and Antwerp. You can choose between a standard visit and a more expensive, detailed tasting session with a beer sommelier.

giddy heights. They mostly have a sweet malt character, delicate European hop notes and a spicy, perfumed quality from the type of yeast used.

Technicalities

Golden ales make a virtue out of just using the palest malt. This may be pale ale malt or even pilsner malt but the key point is that there are no darker malts used, especially crystal malt which normally brings notes of caramel and nut that are not wanted here. Also in the grist may be some wheat malt, to lighten the cereal flavour even further. The beer that ensues is an attractive straw/yellow colour with a crisp, sweet malt base unhindered by richer malt notes. Initially, the British golden ale incorporated English hops – Golding and Challenger were commonly found – but, in a bid to attract lager drinkers, continental hops such as Saaz and Hersbrucker also came into use. In recent times the trend has been to build on the fruitiness by choosing instead American hops such as Cascade and Citra or Australian varieties such as Galaxy. Hops in the Belgian blond style are traditionally more subdued, allowing the sweetness of the malt and the subtle fruit and spice notes created by the yeast during fermentation to share the spotlight. A famous version is Duvel, what you might call a devil of a beer, that deceives the drinker with its strength (8.5% ABV) and has led to many copies since it was perfected in 1970. Recent developments have seen Belgian brewers upping the hop rate in their blonds, adding more of the traditional continental varieties or, like the British brewers, borrowing the exaggerated citrus character of US hops. The mostly Belgian style tripel is also blond but is generally stronger, with a more estery or spicy flavour (see Trappist & abbey beers).

TASTE OFF!

Golden ales

Hop Back Summer Lightning

Gentle citrus fruit is the hallmark of this deceptively drinkable golden ale. Delicate honey and sharp lemon and lime feature in the aroma, with lemon and herb notes in the crisp, marginally bitter taste, before a dry, bitter, herbal-hoppy finish.

Bristol Beer Factory Independence

This golden ale brilliantly showcases the wonders of American hops, bursting with grapefruit and zesty orange fruitiness, backed by tangy, sappy resin notes.

St Stefanus Blonde

The action of the yeast is immediately apparent in the spicy, bready aroma, which has notes of pear, pineapple, melon and a little bubblegum. The taste is mostly sweet, but not overbearing, and there are more spice and tropical fruit notes before a dry, bitter, clove-like finish. A gentle warmth testifies to the 7% ABV of this Belgian blond.

If you want to try more…

… try these other examples:
British Style: Exmoor Gold, Stewart Edinburgh Gold, Wye Valley HPA, Young's London Gold **American Style:** Adnams Ghost Ship, Cheddar Bitter Bully, Harviestoun Bitter & Twisted, Oakham Citra, Sharp's Single Brew Reserve, Vale Gravitas **Belgian Style:** Affligem Blond, Dupont Moinette Blonde, Duvel, Leffe Blond, Malheur 6

… you may also like:
Dortmunder export, heller bock, helles, kölsch, pale ale, pilsner, saison

Strong ales

Strong ale does not really exist as a style. It is more of a convenient grouping for British bitters or pale ales that are stronger than the norm and yet not so dominated by hops as to be judged an India pale ale. In centuries past, such beers would have been totally at home among the pale ales but, as strengths have plummeted in Britain, they now seem a race apart. They are a different drinking experience to best bitters, even though the recipes and flavour components are close. What such beers bring is extra body, a hint of alcoholic warmth and the managed influence of esters – those strange fruity and floral flavours created by yeast in stronger beers. Too weak to be labelled barley wines, they have to sit in this sort of limbo area. They are also a mostly British phenomenon as other countries would not consider the strength of such beers to be in any way high, although in the US there has been a move to emulate one beer in particular, Fuller's ESB, as a mellow contrast to the heavily hop-forward strong pale ales of America.

Technicalities

It's as loose a criterion as you can apply, but strong ales broadly fall into the 4.6–7% ABV bracket. Most are made using the same combinations of pale ale malt, crystal malt, brewing sugar and enhancing adjuncts such as maize and wheat as pale ales and best bitters but, of course, the quantities are greater in order to provide the sugars the yeast can devour to take the strength up to this level. Hops generally come from English farms for a rounded bitterness and restrained fruit and floral notes. A key part of the production process, however, is the fermentation, when brewers need to manage ester creation. Some will wish to harness the esters created during fermentation in order to give their beers a perfumed or fruity edge; others will keep the fermentation temperature lower to minimize such characteristics.

What such beers bring is extra body, a hint of alcoholic warmth and the managed influence of esters

TASTE OFF!

Strong ales

Brakspear Triple

This bottle-conditioned beer used to be a touch stronger and more complex, but it is still a fine example of the post-best bitter/pre-barley wine type of beer that British brewers present. Hints of tropical fruit from Cascade hops are complemented by prominent floral, pear drop and banana notes from fermentation, set against a base of light toffee.

Fuller's ESB

A highly influential beer, ESB has been responsible for a whole new category in American brewing, as US brewers have sought to emulate the full body but restrained English hop character – peppery oranges and a tangy, leafy bitterness – of this London brew that offsets the intrinsic sweetness, subtle floral notes and the faintly caramel-like character of the rich malt.

Greene King Morland Hen's Tooth

A relic from the closed Morland brewery in Oxfordshire, this bottle-conditioned beer has been maintained by Greene King at its Suffolk brewery. It is, as its name suggests, related to the commonly found Old Speckled Hen best bitter but is more subtle and alluring, with lots of pear drop, pineapple and floral notes in the taste.

If you want to try more...

... try these other examples:
Ringwood Old Thumper, Shepherd Neame 1698, Wadworth Old Timer, Young's Special London Ale

... you may also like:
barley wine, bock, India pale ale, pale ale

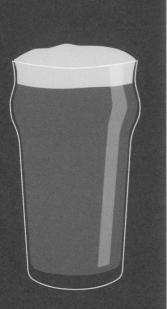

India pale ales

India pale ale (IPA) has been one of the success stories of the last 20 years. It is a style that has been brought back from oblivion, a beer of character that has fuelled the new brewery revolution and has an enchanting story to tell. The only issue is that much of the story of IPA is not true.

In recent times, historians have been actively myth-busting the exaggerated accounts of how the beer was specifically created for the Indian market in the 18th century – a new beer to quench the thirsts of British civil servants, soldiers and merchants living in the sultry subcontinent, one that, unlike existing beers, was designed to withstand the rigours of a testing sea voyage. The truth is still entertaining, although less fanciful.

IPA, it seems, developed quite by chance. There is certainly evidence that some beers shipped to India at that time arrived in poor condition. That was hardly surprising, given that they endured a three- or four-month journey to India, down through the Atlantic, around the tip of Africa on choppy seas in fluctuating temperatures, without refrigeration. But there is also evidence that many beers arrived in perfectly good order and it didn't need to be a special beer to make the journey. As legend has it, the new beer that became known as IPA reached India in fine fettle because it was strong and very hoppy – alcohol and hops both help preserve beer. Yet weaker and less hoppy beers were also exported successfully, meaning that it was a matter of taste and not just better chemical stability that actually made IPA the success it became.

The birth of India pale ale, it appears, can be pinned down to one East London brewer named George Hodgson, who – sometime in the late 1700s – found that his pale-coloured, keeping ale proved popular in India. Hodgson's beer was stylistically known as an October ale, a beer brewed in the autumn, using fresh harvest malt and hops, and then matured for a couple of years. He may have sent a weaker version, as records show his beer to be around 6.5% ABV, and true October beers would have been considerably stronger. Whatever, the long journey, the warm temperatures and the steady rocking of the ocean seemed to accelerate the maturation process, resulting in a beer of character and quality that quickly dominated the profitable Indian market.

Hodgson's successors, however, managed to wreck his strong business. By taking customers for granted and pricing themselves out of the market, they opened the door for the brewers of Burton upon Trent, whose trade in porter with the Baltic nations had been scuppered by Russian tariffs on imported beer.

Today's true IPAs are golden to deep brown in colour and are loaded with hop flavours

The Burton brewers, beginning with Allsopp's, set about re-creating Hodgson's beer and ended up surpassing it, thanks to the naturally hard water their wells provided. From that point onwards, names such as Allsopp, Bass, Salt and Worthington became globally famous for their India pale ales.

Over the 20th century, however, IPA became a lost soul. The trade with India fell away as the sun set on the Empire, and British beers overall became weaker because of duty changes and wartime restrictions. The term IPA was borrowed and abused. It was applied to much weaker beers that peaked at about 3.7% ABV and showed very modest hop character. Some still exist but they have been put in their place by a new generation of more authentic IPAs, beers big on hops and packing a good clout of alcohol.

Today's true IPAs are golden to deep brown in colour and are loaded with hop flavours. That said, variations on the style have developed as the brewing renaissance has taken hold. American brewers have adopted IPA as their badge of honour, but with their local hops employed instead of English. This means the US IPA is a lipsmackingly tangy, fruity cocktail of bountiful hops such as Cascade, Centennial, Chinook and Simcoe. In response, many British brewers now produce their own version of this US style. There has also been the creation of further hybrids such as black and red IPAs, as well as Belgian IPAs, a result of brewers in that country piling hops into their otherwise fairly sweet, spicy blond and amber strong ales.

Technicalities

The beer Hodgson successfully sent to India was known to be pale in colour. While pale malt was not widely used at this time, because coke-fuelled kilns needed to create it were still rare, October ales – typically made on country estates – were known to be produced just from pale malt as this was seen as refined.

When the brewers of Burton upon Trent took up the reins, they found they were able to produce an even better pale beer, one that was both crisper and clearer. This was because the calcium sulphate in the town's natural hard water facilitated better conversion of starches into fermentable sugars and produced less protein haze. Additionally, it takes some harshness away from hop bitterness, causes less colour to leech from the malt into the brewing water (meaning a paler beer can be produced), and helps the yeast to flocculate (clump together and drop to the bottom), leaving a clearer beer. Furthermore, it brings a degree of dryness and crispness, making the beer more refreshing than one made with London's softer water.

Read on

Pete Brown, *Hops and Glory* (Macmillan, 2009)

Clive La Pensée and Roger Protz, *Homebrew Classics: India Pale Ale* (CAMRA Books, 2001)

Mitch Steele, *IPA: Brewing Techniques, Recipes and the Evolution of India Pale Ale* (Brewers Publications, 2012)

Brewers today, wherever they are based, pay homage to the Burton tradition when brewing IPA, treating their brewing water so that it is hard and packed with minerals.

A typical English-style IPA today is made predominantly with pale ale malt, perhaps enriched by a touch of crystal or other darker malt. Hops major on tried-and-tested English varieties such as Fuggle, Golding, Challenger and Target. Across the Atlantic, a kind of hops arms race has hijacked the style, with brewers competing to pack in ever more hops, which are also more pungent and zesty. They've also raised the stakes alcoholically, creating double IPAs or imperial IPAs that have a substantial base of malt and alcohol to support extreme hopping. Weaker beers that borrow the name IPA are really just pale ales/bitters, mostly brewed from pale and crystal malts with English hops such as Fuggle, Golding and Challenger.

Visit

The **National Brewery Centre** (www.nationalbrewerycentre.co.uk) at Burton upon Trent is not just a great introduction to beer in general, it is also a showcase for IPA. The importance of this beer style to the development of the town is there for all to see in displays and hands-on exhibits. Here you can learn about the great Burton brewing families, the importance of the local water and how beer changed the lives of the townsfolk.

TASTE OFF!

India pale ales

Greene King IPA

The prime example of the 20th-century weaker IPA style, a close balance of faintly caramel-like malt and bitter herbal hops, with background notes of apple and suggestions of liquorice. It is bittersweet overall, becoming bitter in the slightly salty finish, and is clearly under-powered and under-hopped compared with traditional IPAs.

Ridgeway IPA

The contrast with Greene King IPA is obvious. This is a much bigger, bolder beer, more typical of a true IPA, although surprisingly quaffable for its 5.5% ABV strength. The hops are much more forceful, bringing zesty bitter orange notes and a light floral character, with sappy hop resins emerging in the dry, bitter orange finish. While the hops are dominant, their flavours are, at the same time, more restrained than in the US version.

Lagunitas IPA

This American IPA is loaded with sappy, fruity hops, giving suggestions of bitter oranges and tangy cucumber peel. You can't hide from the hops but, at the same time, it's a well-balanced drink that becomes eminently quaffable after a striking first few sips.

If you want to try more...

... try these other examples:

'**Weak' IPA:** Caledonian Deuchars IPA, Rebellion IPA, Wadworth Henry's IPA **UK Style:** Burton Bridge Empire Pale Ale, Fuller's Bengal Lancer, Hook Norton Flagship, Meantime IPA, Worthington's White Shield **US Style:** Bristol Beer Factory Southville Hop, Odell IPA, St Austell Proper Job, Sierra Nevada Torpedo, Thornbridge Jaipur

... you may also like:

barley wine, best bitter, dubbel, strong ale

Milds

Mild is one of the most misunderstood beer styles. For the first half of the 20th century it was easily the biggest selling type of beer in the UK, popular particularly among manual workers. The reason they took to mild was that it was the ideal refresher after a hard day of physical toil. It wasn't particularly strong but was rich in unfermented sugars, making it, one could argue, one of the first isotonic drinks. It washed away dust from the throat, replenished liquid lost in sweat and added a little sugar rush to give those workers a spring in their step as they walked home.

Unfortunately, the days of heavy industry in the UK were numbered and, as jobs were lost throughout the 1960s, consumption of mild followed suit. Being a weaker beer than bitter, with fewer hops to disguise off flavours, mild also didn't keep very well once the turnover slowed, and this contributed to its decline, as did the tendency among some brewers to produce a cheap mild by simply colouring a light bitter with caramel.

With the heavy advertising of lager, mild lost further ground until it reached the point in the 1990s when brewers seemed embarrassed to even brew one. If they did, many decided not to describe it as a mild because it had such an unwelcome, old-fashioned image. Thankfully, mild is back. It is not only brewed all over the UK (and in other parts of the world) but is also labelled properly in more and more cases. People are less inclined to turn up their noses at mild and, once they've sampled it, they are often hooked, seduced by its rich malt flavours, its pleasantly low bitterness and its very manageable alcohol content.

Historically, mild's origins date back to at least the 17th century. It's often assumed these days that the style is called mild because it is milder in bitterness than bitter, or milder in alcohol than other beer styles. Both of these things are generally true but historians have pointed out that the term mild is derived from the fact that this was traditionally a fresh beer, served soon after being brewed and therefore picking up none of the sour flavours of beers that had been aged in wood for weeks or months. In essence, it was mild to taste.

The drink we know as mild would have been brewed initially from malt dried over open fires, as the technology for producing pale malt had not yet arrived. So the beer was dark and probably smoky tasting. In time, brewers mellowed the flavour by using the new pale malts and darkening the colour with roasted malts. Hops remained lightly used. Where these early milds differ from most of today's is in strength. A mild in the mid-19th century, for example, generally

The term mild is derived from the fact that this was traditionally a fresh beer, served soon after being brewed

rolled out at the 6–7% ABV mark, whereas today, in most examples, mild offers only around 3–3.5% (a decline instigated by wartime restrictions on malt use and the discouragement of strong alcohol). There are exceptions, however, and strong milds are still in production, many of them recreated from old recipes by adventurous small brewers. There are also milds that are not dark in colour and appear more like bitters in the glass, with a familiar light brown hue.

Technicalities

In recipe, light-coloured milds are basically brewed as low-strength bitters, but fewer hops are used, allowing the malt to shine through. Dark milds are also low in hops, but they tend to include a roasted malt, such as chocolate malt, alongside pale (and often crystal malts) in the mash tun. This adds a chocolate or coffee note to the beer. Some brewers use a type of malt known as mild malt instead of pale malt. It is slightly darker but does the same job. Sometimes sugar is added and another trick to ensure there is plenty of sweetness in mild is to mash the grains at a slightly higher temperature than normal. This results in some of the sugars that are converted from starches not being fermentable by brewers' yeast, so they remain unchanged in the beer instead of being turned into alcohol. Strong milds are mostly dark milds scaled up, ranging from somewhere above 4% ABV to 6% and beyond.

Visit

Most milds are still only available on draught as they lack the alcohol to survive well in a bottle, so take a trip to one of the hotbeds of mild in the UK, such as the West Midlands, where you can not only drink Banks's Mild but milds from Holden's, Hobsons, Bathams and other breweries. Definitely on your hit list should be the **Beacon Hotel** (www.sarahhughesbrewery. co.uk) at Sedgley, near Dudley, where arguably the finest strong mild – Sarah Hughes Dark Ruby (6% ABV) – is brewed and served on draught.

Read on

David Sutula, *Mild Ale* (Brewers Publications, 1999)

TASTE OFF!

Milds

Banks's Mild

This is a Midlands favourite and often surprises drinkers with its light brown colour. It is in the taste that its more obvious connection to the mild world comes through. It's an easy-drinking, bittersweet beer with a low hop character. Notes of creamy caramel and raisin emerge from the malt, with a tannin-like bitterness building eventually in the finish.

Thwaites Nutty Black

In its cask form, this beer is very typically a mild with an ABV of just 3.3%. The bottled version is a touch stronger, at 3.9%, but still exhibits the classic qualities of a British mild ale. Subtle, bittersweet flavours of chocolate and coffee, a pinch of liquorice and some hedgerow fruitiness from the restrained hops define the taste, before a biscuity, roasted grain finish with more liquorice.

Teignworthy Martha's Mild

This beer sums up what strong milds are all about. There is plenty of chocolate and abundant sweetness in the rich malt character, but also berry fruits, a winey note and a touch of warmth from the raised alcohol (5.3%). Chocolate and coffee feature in the full, bittersweet finish.

If you want to try more...

... try these other examples:
Light Milds: McMullen AK, Old Chimneys Ragged Robin, Taylor Golden Best **Dark Milds:** Batemans Black & White, Brains Dark, Cotswold Spring OSM, Hobsons Mild, Hoggleys Mill Lane Mild, Moorhouse's Black Cat, Nobby's Tressler's XXX, Theakston Mild, Vale Black Swan **Strong Milds:** Beowulf Strong Mild, Dark Star Victorian Ruby Mild, Fuller's Gale's Festival Mild, Sarah Hughes Dark Ruby

... you may also like:
brown ale, dubbel, dunkel, old ale, porter, Scotch ale

Brown ales

It is often suggested that brown ale is simply mild put into bottle. That is certainly true in some cases, but the suggestion unravels when you consider that some brown ales have never been sold as milds and that other brown ales are really too hoppy to be described as mild.

There was a time, not so long ago, when it was common to discover little bottles of brown ale behind the bar of your local pub. They were often produced by the parent brewery of the pub and added a bit of variety to the range of cask ales on offer. Customers liked them as beers with a bit more carbonation than cask and drank them on their own or mixed them half-and-half with a mild or a bitter from the handpumps, adding a sparkle of life to a sometimes flat brew. Unfortunately, bottled brown ale fell out of favour at the same time as mild sales were collapsing, during the 1960s and 1970s. Its longevity has also been curbed by brewery rationalization. This means that one-time national brands such as Bass Toby Brown, Watney's Brown Ale and Whitbread's Forest Brown are no more, and neither are regional equivalents such as Holdens Brown Ale, Shepherd Neame Brown Ale and Tolly Cobbold Cobnut. There are, however, some notable survivors.

The oldest known brown ale still in production is Manns Brown Ale. This was introduced in 1902. Manns' Whitechapel brewery has long gone and, in the machinations of brewery mergers and takeovers, the beer has found its way into the hands of Marston's and is brewed in Burton upon Trent. Manns is the archetypal southern brown ale. At just 2.8% ABV, it sits at the low end of beer's alcoholic spectrum but it does not lack flavour. Its mostly sweet, malty taste (generally sweeter than many milds) contrasts with the more robust flavours of a northern (probably better referred to as north-eastern) brown ale, a style best exemplified by the globally successful Newcastle Brown Ale. First produced in 1927, this beer has gained a cult following among rockers and bikers, but beer connoisseurs are not usually impressed, possibly because, being pasteurized and sold in clear glass bottles – and rarely in its history offered in cask form – it is not always tasted at its peak. Nevertheless, it is easy to spot the difference between this and the southern style of brown ale. Not only is Newcastle Brown lighter in colour and stronger (4.7% ABV) but it is also hoppier. Other examples of this northern style are now in circulation, but there are very few of the southern equivalent around as the style has been passed over in favour of mild.

A new dimension to brown ale has arrived with the new brewery movement in the US. In America, where Newcastle Brown is a commonly found import,

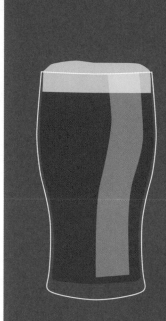

There was a time, not so long ago, when it was common to discover little bottles of brown ale behind the bar of your local pub

Read on

Ray Daniels and Jim Parker,
Brown Ale (Brewers
Publications, 1988)

they have taken the basic principle and boosted it with a little more alcohol and the addition of fragrant American hops, giving the new drink a floral and fruity accent.

Technicalities

Four centuries or more ago, many beers on sale would have been considered brown ales, as the malt used in those days had been dried over fires and had a charred nature, so colouring the beer. They would also have been strong, 6% ABV and above, in the fashion of the time. But this style of beer was soon abandoned by the drinking public in favour of porters and then pale ales. What we today know as southern-style brown ales were introduced with the arrival of Manns in the early 20th century. While the recipe includes crystal malt and some roasted malt, a key feature is sugary sweetness, created by not fully fermenting the beer and thus preventing the yeast from eating up all the sugars.

Northern-style brown ales do not generally use roasted grains but have a malt grist comprising pale and crystal malts, perhaps with a dab of caramel for colour (although, owing to public pressure in the US, brand owner Heineken dropped caramel from the recipe for Newcastle Brown in 2015). They are much drier, because the fermentation is more complete, and they also have a greater hop presence, leading to more bitterness in the taste. The American-style brown ale often falls somewhere between the two English styles, being dark with a touch of roasted grain (either dark malt or roasted barley), sweet but also hoppy, thanks to the inclusion of fruity varieties such as Mount Hood, Cascade and Citra.

TASTE OFF!

Brown ales

Manns Brown Ale

This dark ruby beer is quite lean, as you would expect from the modest 2.8% alcohol, but it doesn't short-change you in flavour. Crystal and black malts bring notes of caramel and bitter chocolate throughout and there's a noticeable sugary note. Bitterness grows in the finish as both hops and roasted grains push through.

Samuel Smith Nut Brown Ale

Dark copper-red in colour, this northern beer is far more robust than Manns. Bitterness is obvious, thanks to the tangy, tea-like hop notes that lead the way. Underneath are the malt contributions, mostly soft caramel and toffee, plus a touch of walnut to confirm the beer's name. Esters bring suggestions of almonds and banana, then toasted grains leave a dry, bitter, biscuity and mildly toffee-like finish.

Brooklyn Brown Ale

Nutty, chocolate-like malts dominate this easy-drinking, ruby-brown beer, which is not as fruity as some American brown ales but nevertheless does reveal a distinct US hop influence in the aroma and taste. Overall, it is bittersweet and rich, with roasted grains leaving a nutty, coffee finish.

If you want to try more...

... try these other examples:
Southern Style: Harveys Bloomsbury Brown
Northern Style: Holts Manchester Brown Ale, Maxim Double Maxim, Newcastle Brown Ale **US Style:** Anchor Brekle's Brown, Nøgne Ø Brown Ale, Thwaites Big Ben, Willy Good Willy Brown

... you may also like:
dubbel, dunkel, mild, old ale, porter, Scotch ale

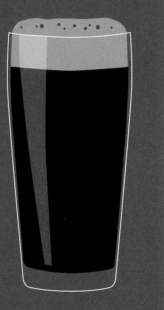

Stouts & porters

Stout and porter came into existence in London in the early 1700s but, if the fogs of the capital at that time have become notorious, they are as nothing compared with the stygian mists that obscure the true origins of these particular beer styles.

Fanciful tales are related about how a publican named Ralph Harwood created porter. His customers, we are told, demanded that he serve a mix of three different beers in one mug, causing Harwood to run between casks to give his customers what they called 'three threads'. To save time, and a lot of messing about in the taproom, he decided to brew a beer that provided all the flavour of the three beers in one cask. He called the beer entire butt, because the entire beer was, so to speak, in one butt (or cask). This became shortened to entire, until the popularity of the new brew among London's street porters saw it renamed after them.

Harwood was indeed a real person but the fact is he lived too late to be in at the creation of porter and his importance to the story has been downgraded in favour of a more prosaic reason for the development of the drink. Previously, it seems, the most popular drink of the day was sweet brown ale. Then brewers extended their repertoire by developing a more bitter beer, a beer that incorporated more hops and also had a greater roasted, smoky character, from malts that had been dried over ferociously hot wood fires. Brewers found that this smoke flavour dissipated when the beer was allowed to age and so they began maturing the beer in wooden casks. Unfortunately, this was in the days before the technology existed to combat wild yeast and bacteria, and the ageing process allowed those intruders time to get to work in the beer, resulting in sourness and acidity affecting many batches. So the choice was to drink beer young but smoky or smoke-free but often sour. A third way – if you didn't care for the first two options – was to blend young and mature versions together and this is how porter progressed and became favoured by the aforementioned workers who gave it their name. Porter also came in a stronger, or stouter, version, appropriately called stout porter but soon abbreviated to stout.

Over the 19th and 20th centuries, porter and stout changed complexion, thanks to improvements in malting and other factors. With the increasing availability of pale malt, which provided a better sugar yield than smoky brown malts, brewers tampered with recipes, making porter and stout with a high proportion of pale malt, perhaps some amber malt, and then just a little dark malt

Porter also came in a stronger, or stouter, version, appropriately called stout porter but soon abbreviated to stout

for colour and flavour. A new highly roasted black malt, known as patent malt, also became a useful ingredient and gradually took over from other coloured malts. The ageing process was no longer required and so matured porter became less important.

However, this was the time when pale ale was rapidly gaining popularity and brewers soon began ripping out their porter tuns and switching production to the beer of the moment. Porter also slowly became weaker and, by the time of the World War I, with its restrictions on malt use, its strength became significantly reduced, dropping in some cases to around 3.5% ABV. The style never recovered, giving further ground to stout which, although itself also significantly weaker than before, remained a touch stronger. Porter production petered out. It needed the brewery revival of the 1980s to see porter back on the bars of British pubs. Over time, stout and porter had become different beasts, stout becoming dryer and more bitter, thanks to the greater use of patent black malt instead of brown – a move that was adopted particularly by Irish brewers. The replacement of roasted malt with roasted barley during the 20th century also firmed up the

Insight

The way porter production developed meant that the style became the first mass-market beer, one that gave its brewers economy-of-scale advantages over producers of other beers. Brewers – as historian Martyn Cornell points out in his book *Amber, Gold & Black* – discovered that porter could be fermented at a higher temperature than other beers, meaning that – in those pre-refrigeration days – it could be brewed for longer periods of the year and also in larger batches (a large volume of beer produces more heat during fermentation). Brewers such as Whitbread and Truman made their fortunes by realizing this.

At the height of its popularity *porter was matured* in huge tuns

character of the dry Irish stout, adding another dimension to the stout and porter story, which had already generated a number of style variations.

Apart from fresh and matured beers already described, there were also sweet versions, in which bitterness remained low. Oatmeal stout arrived in the late 19th century, with oats (malted or unmalted) added to the grist for a creamier flavour and a smoother texture. Then there were also milk stouts, reinforced by the addition not of milk but of milk sugar (lactose). Lactose cannot be fermented by brewers' yeast and so contributes sweetness and body to the beer. Both sweet and milk stouts mostly sat at the lower end of the alcohol scale but stout and porter were also pushing the top end.

For export, a strong variety of stout proved successful. Well hopped for preservative effect and heavy in alcohol – anything from around 7.5% to 10% and above – the beer was shipped around the world. Some of the strongest proved popular across the Baltic Sea where it was lapped up by frozen aristocrats in the Russian imperial court. Imperial Russian stout, as it was called, then spawned a copycat in the breweries of eastern Europe, a brew that became known as Baltic porter and was, in some instances, bottom fermented and cold conditioned – in other words, a lager equivalent. With the revival of all these styles in recent years, we can now enjoy beers that may be sweet, creamy, dry, full bodied, mildly alcoholic or vinously strong – in short, the full rainbow of stout and porter creations. Dark beer is more colourful than you think.

Technicalities

The early name for porter, entire butt, was probably coined not in the pub by Ralph Harwood but in the brewhouse and for a different reason than because the beer combined elements of three different beers in one cask. A likely origin lies in the fact that the beer was made by mashing the same grains several times and blending together all the extracts, from the sugar-richest to the thinnest – unlike in other beers where only the extract from the first mash would be used to make the strongest beers and later, thinner mashes using the same grain went to make weaker beers. With the beer then matured for months in giant butts – to lessen the smokiness of its taste – it gained the name entire butt, or entire for short. Brewing water for porter and stout does not need to be as hard as for pale ales. This meant that centres such as London and Dublin, with their carbonate-rich water, were able to prosper from porter and stout brewing when they would have struggled to compete with pale ale centres such as Burton upon Trent. A typical recipe for porter in the early 19th century would have comprised around 78% pale malt and 22% brown malt. Soon, the arrival of black patent malt meant that less brown malt (around 6%) and more pale malt (around 90%) were used, with the black malt providing nearly all the colour and much of the roasted flavour from just about 3 or 4% of the grist. Recipes, generally speaking, are not much different today, but there may be more use of chocolate malt and less use of black malt, certainly in porters. Stouts, originally, were just scaled-up versions of porter recipes, but today's dry Irish stout brewers may include around 8% or more roasted barley.

Being overwhelmed by the dark flavours of the malt, hops in porters and stouts play a secondary role, traditionally being employed for their preservative quality and their bitterness, rather than richness of flavour. Consequently, less strident varieties such as Fuggle and Northdown have been popular choices. That has changed in the modern era, when some breweries like to use pungent New World hops to add another dimension to their stouts and porters.

The difference between porter and stout today is as vague as the origin of the beers itself, with the strengths tending to be roughly equal. As a loose generalization, it can perhaps be said that today's porters are a little sweeter and lighter in body than today's stouts, often with a more chocolate-like taste. But, given the variety of sweet, dry, oatmeal, milk and imperial stouts and porters described earlier, there can be no hard and fast guidance.

Read on

Terry Foster, *Porter* (Brewers Publications, 1992)

Clive La Pensée and Roger Protz, *Homebrew Classics Stout & Porter* (CAMRA Books, 2003)

Michael J Lewis, *Stout* (Brewers Publications, 1995)

Roger Protz, *Classic Stout & Porter* (Prion Books, 1997)

Visit

More a celebration of the brand than stout itself, and aimed squarely at general tourists, a visit to the **Guinness Storehouse** at St James's Gate, Dublin (www. guinness-storehouse.com) nevertheless explores the history of the business and the importance of stout to Ireland. And it gives you a nice retro look at those great Guinness adverts, too.

TASTE OFF!

Stouts & porters

Moncada Notting Hill Porter

This deep ruby beer features lots of roasted grains but still has that lightness of body and initial sweetness that mark it out as a porter from a dry Irish stout. Coffee and chocolate flavours fill the palate, with the roasted grain leaving more coffee in the pleasantly bitter finish.

Hook Norton Double Stout

This garnet-coloured dry stout features black malt that not only deepens the colour but also helps build more bitterness than found in the Moncada porter. Lighter touches are provided by notes of milk chocolate, coffee and caramel, and a hint of pear-like fruit. Roasted grain takes over in the dry, bitter finish.

Bristol Beer Factory Milk Stout

Sweet coffee and contrasting bitter chocolate are the key features of this deep burgundy beer. The added lactose ensures a creamy richness and also a sugary note, but this is countered by burnt grains and some tangy hops.

Wells Courage Imperial Russian Stout

The alcohol is immediately evident in this heady, very dark beer, a true throwback to the early years of the style. Laced around it are notes of coffee, liquorice and a hint of caramel, with suggestions of orange providing a little contrast and sugared almond notes developing as the beer warms in the mouth. The gum-tingling finish is firmly dry and biscuity with roasted grains pushing through to leave coffee and bitter chocolate on the palate.

Zywiec Baltic Porter

This great survivor – an eastern European response to the imperial stout – is a deep ruby lager, with an oily-smooth texture and a predominantly sweet, vinous taste. Creamy, bitter chocolate and raisins also feature, continuing into the dry, warming finish where hops emerge in young versions to compete with the lingering dark chocolate.

Flying Dog Gonzo Imperial Porter

This near-black American take on the style is a potent, uninhibited contest between piney, fruity hop resins – grapefruit and orange to the fore – and dark chocolate notes from the smoky roasted grains. Those US hops just shade it.

... try these other examples:

Porter: Chiltern The Lord Lieutenant's Porter, Elland 1872 Porter, Otley 06 Porter, RCH Old Slug Porter, Wickwar Station Porter **Dry Stout:** Guinness Original, Hop Back Entire Stout, Wye Valley Dorothy Goodbody's Wholesome Stout **Milk Stout:** Left Hand Milk Stout, Mackeson Stout **Imperial Stout:** Acorn Gorlovka, Durham Temptation, Harveys Imperial Extra Double Stout, The Kernel Export Stout, Thornbridge Saint Petersburg **Baltic Porter:** Baltika 6, Hopshackle Baltic Porter, Okocim Porter, Synebrychoff Koff Porter

If you want to try more...

... you may also like:

dunkel, mild, rauchbier, schwarzbier

Traditional old ales tend to be full bodied and rather strong

Old ales

A couple of centuries ago, old ale was a straightforward proposition. It literally meant strong ale that had been allowed to mature in oak casks for a year or two (possibly longer). The process had notable consequences, not least the fact that the beer would often pick up wild yeast and bacterial infections, resulting in it becoming acidic and sour. But that's the way people liked it, especially when blended with a younger, fresher beer.

For the best surviving example of a traditional old ale in the UK we can look to Greene King. At the Bury St Edmunds brewery, the company ages one particular beer in giant oak casks. The beer is given the name 5X and to sample it neat is a rare treat as it is rarely publicly sold. The taste is sugary sweet but countered by a gentle tartness imparted from the long exposure to oak. Usually, however, the beer is used for blending to create a beer called Strong Suffolk. The blending takes away some of the original character but the effect of ageing is still apparent in the taste. A fairly recent development has been to blend 5X with Old Speckled Hen to create a second beer, called Old Crafty Hen.

Another notable old ale in the historic mould is Prize Old Ale, which Fuller's acquired when it took over the Gale's brewery in Hampshire. This famous, bottle-conditioned beer had been brewed since the 1920s and Fuller's has continued to produce it at Chiswick (although less frequently of late). Otherwise, for a taste of the past, you have to look to other countries, and Belgium in particular, where the concept of ageing beer for many months remains very popular because, in the UK, old ale has developed into a rather different beast. The ageing has gone and the style is more or less seen just as a dark, modestly hopped beer of a reasonable strength. Many old ales are brewed just for the winter months. Fruity, winey and smoky flavours may be present, but acidity and sourness are seldom found.

Technicalities

Traditional old ales tended to be full bodied and rather strong (to help them age well). They were also relatively pale in colour, in contrast with the porters of the day, but recipes varied. Greene King's 5X (around 12% ABV), for instance, is constructed from a grist of pale malt, a little roasted malt and cane sugar, with various English hops for balance. Gale's Prize Old Ale (9% ABV) takes pale, crystal and chocolate malt and seasons the wort with Fuggle and Golding hops. The key for both beers is, of course, the ageing process – up to two years for 5X and up to a year for Gale's. Both beers are then blended. 5X is combined with a younger, weaker beer called BPA (which itself is never sold neat) to create Strong Suffolk, which runs out at 6% ABV. For Gale's, the blending is with a younger version of Prize Old Ale.

Belgium's oud bruin ('old brown'), native to the town of Oudenaarde and its environs, is brewed to the same principles and again blended with younger beer for commercial sale. Its close cousin (if there is any difference between them) is the Flemish red style, headed up by the beers from Rodenbach brewery in Roeselare. The beers Rodenbach produces are made using a mix of pale and coloured malts, with some maize. The wort is boiled with hops that are a couple of years old – hop flavour is not wanted in this beer, only the natural preservative qualities of the hops. After fermentation and a month of conditioning in a tank, the beer is transferred into giant wooden tuns known as foeders where it sits, undisturbed, for up to two years at around 15ºC (59ºF). During this time, the porosity of the oak allows in some oxygen, which is seized on by microflora resident in the wood to create fruity esters and turn the beer acidic. After its two years, the beer is flat and extremely tart, with a pH (acidity level) of around 3.3. A normal beer has a pH of just over 4.0. Blending with an unaged version of the same beer reduces the acidity and provides some sweetness. The standard product is Rodenbach Classic (5% ABV), in which young beer is blended with old at a ratio of 3:1, making it fruity and gently sour but very quaffable. The premium product is Rodenbach Grand Cru (6% ABV), which is two parts beer from the foeder and one part young beer. It is notably sour, acetic and challenging, despite also being sweetened.

The modern version of old ale in the UK is very similar to a strong mild, often made from pale, crystal and another roasted malt and softly laced with English hops. The strength is around 5% ABV and above – although some examples are weaker – and esters are often encouraged, to bring berry and tropical fruit notes. There is very little ageing to talk about at the brewery but this doesn't prevent the beers from having plenty of character.

Insight

When it took over Prize Old Ale, Fuller's was able to use the final brew produced at Gale's, which was still maturing in tank. It bottled most of this but held some back to blend into the second batch, which would be brewed at Fuller's and, ever since, it has cleverly recreated the character of the Gale's beer by keeping back a quantity of each brew for blending into the next. Through this process, the original Gale's bacteria stay active in the beer, turning brew after brew naturally acidic. If you can lay hands on the 2007 vintage, the full power of wood ageing will be laid before you in the shockingly tart, fruity taste. Later vintages have been blended differently. They are much sweeter and acceptable to more palates.

Visit

Rodenbach's brewery (www.rodenbach.be) in Roeselare is open for group visits. These take in not just the brewhouse but also, very importantly, the maturation cellar packed with nearly 300 enormous foeders filled with beer (right). It is an awesome sight and some of these vessels are more than 150 years old. If you can't get to Belgium, **CAMRA's National Winter Ales Festival** (nwaf. org.uk) is held every January/ February in different locations in the UK. There, old ales – mostly of the modern kind – take their place among barley wines, stouts and porters. Also check out the **Old Ale Festival** held every November at The White Horse pub (www.whitehorsesw6.com) in Parsons Green, London, where dozens of old ales from the UK and further afield are showcased in an event that has been run for more than 30 years.

TASTE OFF!

Old ales

Theakston Old Peculier

Exemplifying the current concept of an old ale, Old Peculier is a deep ruby beer with faintly winey aromas and flavours of berries, bramble fruits and liquorice, on a sweet, but never cloying, malt base.

Greene King Strong Suffolk

A blended old ale in the historic style, this is a bittersweet, ruby beer with caramel, tart fruit and hints of liquorice and apple in the slightly sugary taste, with the wood ageing bringing an oaky, drying tang at all times and a just a hint of acidic sourness to freshen things up.

Rodenbach Grand Cru

Almost claret in colour, this Belgian beer grabs your attention with the first sniff, as vinous, tart fruit notes dominate the aroma. One sip sets the tastebuds alive with sharp fruit, oak and plenty of acidity that burns the throat as you swallow, leaving a dry, tart, fruity finish.

If you want to try more...

... try these other examples:
Modern: Downton Chimera Dark Delight, Moor Old Freddy Walker, Robinson's Old Tom **Traditional:** Fuller's Gale's Prize Old Ale **Oud bruin/Flemish red:** Ichtegems Oud Bruin, Liefmans Goudenband, Petrus Oud Bruin, Verhaeghe Duchesse de Bourgogne

... you may also like:
Modern: barley wine, doppelbock, porter, Scotch ale, strong mild
Traditional/oud bruin/Flemish red: Berliner weisse, gueuze, lambic

The style has also picked up a transatlantic cousin

Barley wines

Barley wine and old ale are very close cousins. Some experts argue that they are just slight variations of the same style, as both can be matured for long periods, but an expectation has developed that barley wine should be notably stronger than most old ales, and paler in colour, although that is by no means a given. Very often, whether a beer is a barley wine or an old ale depends simply on what the brewer decides to call it.

The history of barley wine dates back to the country estates of 18th-century England, to the days when pale malt was beginning to make its presence known to brewers. Strong ales were brewed every autumn from freshly harvested barley and hops and were kept to mature for a year or two (and longer). These so-called October ales were helped from turning sour by the heavy hopping they were given – hops, as I have shown, acting as a natural preservative in beer. The nobility particularly enjoyed them after their meals, as a cheaper (and perhaps more patriotic) alternative to brandy, which was being heavily taxed at the time. This is probably how the alternative name of barley wine came into use, although there is no evidence of brewers widely using that term until the end of the 19th century. For much of the 20th century barley wine – like other strong beers – suffered a major decline, as taxation and malt restrictions due to war impacted on the brewing industry. The only brand with any kind of prominence was Whitbread's Gold Label, but that has now been well overshadowed by the revival of the barley wine style. Many breweries have been encouraged to create or rediscover their own barley wines by the revival of the bottled beer market, which lends itself to a style of beer that is not so easy to sell on draught. The style has also picked up a transatlantic cousin as American brewers have taken the concept and laced it generously with their distinctive local hops.

Technicalities

One of the most acclaimed British barley wines of the last 200 years has been Bass No. 1. Brewed in Burton upon Trent, this was a 10.5% ABV beer of immense character, as was shown when it was revived in the 1990s by the small brewery in the Bass Museum (today's National Brewery Centre). The feisty strength of the beer was built on wort chock-full of brewing sugars that became even more concentrated during a long copper boil that evaporated the liquid. When recreated at the Museum, the boil lasted 12 hours, reducing five barrels of wort down to three, and was responsible for turning the appearance of the beer dark amber, even though only pale malt was used in the mash. It is fair to assume that other such strong beers in the past would also have been boiled for longer than the norm.

Barley wine is not extensively aged at the brewery these days, but it does mature magnificently in the bottle, especially if bottle conditioned. Tastings of Fuller's Vintage Ale, which is brewed once a year and dated, have shown how beers 15 years old are not just still drinkable but have also gained new qualities not evident in their younger equivalents, as the hop character has faded and oxidation has introduced notes of fortified wine.

A typical barley wine today would be made with pale malt and perhaps a little crystal or other darker malt, but generally not using the roasted grains that feature in today's old ales. Hops would be English, with Fuggle, Challenger and Golding popular choices and the likes of Centennial, Chinook and Cascade substituting for these in the US. Fermentation flavours are allowed to develop, so the fruitiness of the hops is complemented by fruit esters from the action of the yeast.

Visit

CAMRA's National Winter Ales Festival (nwaf.org.uk), held every January/February (venues vary), presents an invitation to try dozens of barley wines, alongside old ales, stouts and porters, including those considered the best in the Champion Winter Beer of Britain competition, which is judged at the event. To indulge in American-style barley wines, San Francisco's **Toronado bar** (www.toronado. com) is the place to head every February, when its **Barleywine Festival** runs for a couple of days.

TASTE OFF!

Barley wines

Coniston No. 9

This dark golden ale features lots of stewed apple and grape fruitiness, with floral esters emerging in the smooth, sweet taste and hops adding a grassy, tangy bitterness to the dry finish.

Hopshackle Restoration

This chestnut-coloured beer is mostly sweet and filled with juicy tropical fruit notes, with pineapple and berries in the mix. Cola and cough candy flavours provide a backdrop before a dry, gently warming, bittersweet finish. The body is light because of the use of brewing sugar.

Anchor Old Foghorn

An American take on the style. This is a sumptuous light ruby beer with peppery, piney hop resins and hints of pineapple and sarsaparilla in the aroma and the warming, bittersweet taste. Tangy US hops take over in the drying, increasingly bitter finish.

If you want to try more…

… try these other examples:
British: Chiltern Bodgers Barley Wine, Durham Benedictus, Fuller's Vintage Ale, Green Jack Ripper, Hogs Back A over T, Lees Harvest Ale, Quantock UXB **US:** AleSmith Old Numbskull, Rogue XS Old Crustacean, Sierra Nevada Bigfoot

… you may also like:
bock, doppelbock, old ale, strong ale, tripel

Pale lagers

Once people have got over the sometimes gobsmacking revelation that the difference between an ale and a lager is nothing to do with colour, and that all lagers are not yellow, they can embark on a journey into one of the most fascinating areas in the beer world. As they do so, they begin to discover that this is where some of the most refreshing and satisfying of beers can be found.

As discussed earlier, lager beers are typified by being fermented at a lower temperature than ales and then being cold-conditioned for a matter of weeks, if not months. The strain of yeast that is used performs slowly but well under such conditions. It likes to sink to the bottom of the fermenting wort, rather than float on the top, when it has completed its work, and it produces a beer that is crisp and clean, rather than chewy and estery. Those are the technical traits that bind beers from the lager world together, but these beers can differ markedly in terms of recipe, strength, colour and flavour. That said, most lagers are generally pale in colour, with very lightly cured malt at the core of the recipe.

The first golden lager was created in Pilsen, in today's Czech Republic, in 1842. The story has it that the local beer was so bad that the townsfolk banded together and funded a new brewery, installing a brewer from Bavaria named Josef Groll. He brought with him the newly honed technique of bottom fermentation and, abandoning the darker malts that had characterized previous Pilsen beers, he created a golden brew, taking advantage of new pale-coloured malts – such as were being used in the UK to make pale ale – and the soft local water. The pilsener or pilsner style, as it became known (the name meaning 'from Pilsen'), proved instantly popular and rapidly raced across country borders, becoming the most emulated in the entire world.

In its Czech homeland, pilsner is a term only used for beer from Pilsen but beers broadly in this style from other Czech towns are similarly known for their rich malt character, based on high-quality, low-nitrate barley from the Moravia region, and their pronounced hop flavour, ringing with the herbal notes of the local Saaz hop. In Germany, pilsner (also abbreviated to pils) is somewhat different from its Czech cousin. It is often a touch lighter in body and the hop character is more sharp and sherbety or floral, with German hops adding their influence. In the north of Germany, pils is also much drier, with a good smack of hops throughout, especially in the quenching finish. Such beers are often described as 'herb' on the labels. It simply means dry. Unfortunately, in other countries, the name pilsner has been widely abused, particularly by some of the largest breweries. Their beers often have little in common with the original pilsner, apart from colour. Adjuncts often take the place of quality malt and the hops – if you can find them – are dull and dreary. Thankfully, a new generation of brewers, all across the world, is now returning pilsner to its rightful place in the brewing pantheon.

Germany was also responsible for taking golden lager and developing it in different directions. In Bavaria, the most favoured style is helles; the name means pale. It is less hoppy than pilsner and is often just known to locals as 'bier'. Brewed by hundreds of long-established, family breweries in towns all across the region, it is the equivalent of local bread from trusted family bakeries, consumed as a matter of daily life. What makes it special is the fact that the beer is so fresh. Usually, it is not pasteurized and has travelled only a few miles to its point of sale. With its abundance of sweet malt flavours and delicate balance of bitterness from hops that also bring hints of lemon or perfume, helles is a supremely refreshing beer that you can drink all evening.

A slightly darker lager is märzen. In 16th-century Germany it was decreed that brewing in the summer months was not allowed because of the danger of bacteria spoiling the beer. March was the last full month in which brewing was permitted and so, märzen, or March beer, was a general term given to a beer that had been brewed in the early spring and safely stored in a cool place throughout the following summer. The specific style known as märzen originated in the early 19th century and, because of the timing of its release, became closely associated with the Munich Oktoberfest. Inspired by a reddish-coloured lager created by Anton Dreher in Vienna (see Dark lagers), it originally poured darker than the deep golden colour most examples present today, but the full malt notes remain, Märzen being a little stronger and richer than helles and pilsner.

Further north in Germany, the industrial city of Dortmund also put its stamp on the pale lager style. There, in the 19th century, brewers created their equivalent of helles, instilling more body but a drier character. It was less aromatic than pilsner and – being quenching and easy to drink – appealed to the local coalminers and steelworkers. It was also sold widely outside of the city, and became known as export as a result. Unfortunately, Dortmund's brewing heritage has collapsed. There used to be two prime producers in the city, both known by their initials: DUB – Dortmunder Union Brauerei – and DAB – Dortmunder Actien Brauerei. Both are now brand names of the Dr Oetker/Radeberger group and both their exports are brewed at the DAB brewery.

Read on

David Miller, *Continental Pilsner* (Brewers Publications, 1990)

Evan Rail, *Good Beer Guide Prague & the Czech Republic* (CAMRA Books, 2007)

Steve Thomas, *Good Beer Guide Germany* (CAMRA Books, 2006)

TASTE OFF!

Pale lagers

Augustiner Lagerbier Hell

This beer sums up how wonderfully quaffable the helles style can be. It's a soft, elegant, easy-drinking, bittersweet blend of sweet lemon, gentle herbs and perfumed hops that leaves a moreish, lipsmackingly tangy finish, without going overboard on the hops.

Dortmunder Union Export

This looks the same as a helles, bright yellow in the glass, and many of the same flavour characteristics are here too, particularly lemon and herbs. But this is a notably drier beer and a touch more bitter.

Rothaus Eis Zäpfle

Described as a märzen export, this beer from the Black Forest does not have the deep golden/amber colouring of an original märzen but certainly offers the fullness of body and the strength to fit the style. Silky, thick malt layers the palate, topped with herbal hops and some distinct fermentation flavours such as almond before a dry, perfumed, bitter finish. It's much bigger and more powerful than a helles or an export, and less crisp and sharp than a German pils.

Pilsner Urquell

The classic Czech Pilsner, this rich golden-coloured beer has a notably creamy, some say buttery, character, partly derived from the sweet malt and partly, it seems, from a touch of diacetyl. On top of this is powerful, herbal hop flavour that dominates the big, dry, creamy finish.

Weihenstephaner Pilsner

It looks similar to Pilsner Urquell but this typically German pils is a much crisper, drier and leaner beer, with more sweetness in the malt to balance the slightly perfumed, herbal hops. There's more perfume in the firmly dry, bitter, herbal-hop finish.

Jever Pilsener

Although again clear gold in colour, and offering lots of peppery, herbal hops, what defines the best-known example of a northern German pilsner is the drying backnote in the taste and then uncompromising dryness in the long-lasting bitter, peppery, herbal-hoppy finish.

If you want to try more...

... try these other examples:

Helles: Fordham Helles Lager, Hofbräu Original, Paulaner Original Münchener Hell **Dortmunder Export:** DAB, Great Lakes Dortmunder Gold, Svyturys Ekstra **Märzen:** Ayinger Oktoberfest-Märzen, Hacker-Pschorr Oktoberfest-Märzen **Czech Pilsner:** Bernard Svetly Lezak, Budweiser Budvar, Windsor & Eton Republika, Zatec **German Pilsner:** Ganter Pilsner, Veltins Pilsner, Waldhaus Diplom Pils, Weltenburger Pils **Northern German Pilsner:** Birrificio Italiano Tipopils, Holsten Extra Herb

... you may also like:

bock, golden ale, kölsch

Visit

Pilsner Urquell
(pilsnerurquell.com) – the
name means original source
Pilsner – is rightly proud
of its status as the world's
first golden lager and
commemorates the fact with
an excellent brewery tour.
Visitors can not only see
the beer in production but
also take a walk through the
history of the beer, viewing
the original kettle that
produced the first beer and
winding up with a tasting of
unfiltered beer from large
oak casks in the cold, dark
cellars – a flavour of the way
the beer used to be made
before modern technology
took over. Also in the town
is the **Brewery Museum**
(www.prazdrojvisit.cz), where
artefacts of the old days are
stored and beer's importance
to this part of the Czech
Republic is illustrated. Another
excellent Czech brewery tour
can be enjoyed at **Budweiser
Budvar** (www.visitbudvar.cz)
in Ceské Budejovice, where
they proudly defend their
90-day lagering methods.

Technicalities

The prerequisites of good pale lager brewing are soft water, quality light-coloured malt, classic European hops and an efficient, bottom-fermenting yeast strain. The soft water guarantees a smooth mouthfeel and ensures flinty mineral notes don't get in the way of the clean malt and hop flavours. The lager malt used (as well as the even paler pilsner malt) is lighter in colour than the pale ale malt used in golden ales. For a slightly darker colour and a touch more body, malts such as Munich and Vienna may also be used. Traditionally, because of the low quality of the malt available, brewers used decoction mashing to extract as much fermentable sugar as possible from poorly modified grain. Usually, this was double decoction, meaning parts of the wort were transferred twice from the mash mixer to the mash cooker, but some brewers adopted triple decoction, with three transfers. Many lager brewers today use a simple temperature-programmed mash system, without decoction.

Hops such as Saaz from the Czech Republic, and Tettnanger, Spalt, Perle and Hallertauer Mittelfrüh from Germany, maintain a traditional herbal flavour although, with brewers constantly experimenting, pale lagers are being brewed with fruitier and more floral hops in other parts of the world. *Saccharomyces pastorianus* yeast ferments the wort and then chips away at the green beer, working steadily during cold conditioning to purge the rougher elements.

The original pilsner beer comes from Pilsner Urquell, Josef Groll's old brewery. The strength of the beer is surprisingly modest, at 4.4% ABV, as most other premium Czech pilsner-type beers are stronger, around 5%. German pils offers about 4.8% ABV and helles around 5%, while Dortmunder export is about 5% or a little more. Märzen runs between 5.5 and 6% ABV. In recent times, some brewers (mostly in the US) have begun producing imperial pilsners that have strengths in the region of 7–9%.

Because of the delicacy of pale lager, care must be taken with packaging and, sadly, many Czech and German pale lagers suffer at the hands of the pasteurizer when bottled. The best experiences undoubtedly come when drinking the beer fresh and unpasteurized close to the place of origin.

Pilsner Urquell is best enjoyed fresh and *unpasteurized* in Pilsen

Dark lagers

While Josef Groll may take the plaudits for creating the world's first golden lager, what he achieved was perhaps not much more than a natural progression from results achieved by other brewers. In particular, the work of Anton Dreher in Vienna and Gabriel Sedlmayer in Munich was already pointing the way towards Groll's great breakthrough.

Dreher and Sedlmayer were good friends and travelling buddies. They were, it transpires, also industrial spies who stole the secrets of English pale ale brewers and others and used them to their own advantage. The two had visited the UK gathering brewing knowledge, surreptitiously acquiring samples of wort and yeast that they hid in a hollow walking stick. When they returned home to their respective cities, they set about putting into practice the lessons they had learned.

Dreher was inspired by the lighter malts he had encountered on his trip and saw a market for a lager that was not – like every other lager on the market – muddy brown in colour, because of the crude method of drying the malt over smoky flames. Creating a paler malt which came to be known as Vienna malt, he launched a lager in 1841 that, while nowhere near as bright and yellow as Groll's was to be a year later, was considerably paler than other beers around. It was light red in colour and, it seems, had a spicy, toasted flavour. However, Groll's pilsner beer soon outstripped Dreher's Vienna lager in popularity and the latter fell into decline, even in its own country. Indeed, it was only kept alive in Mexico, of all places, which was a once far-flung outpost of the Austrian empire. Happily, Vienna has now been revived and is once again gaining popularity around the world.

Sedlmayer, too, made the most of his travelling experience. His Spaten brewery developed a similar, lighter-coloured malt which became known as Munich malt. This was then used to perfect the amber-coloured märzen style of lager although, as we have seen, most märzens today tend to be much paler.

Vienna and (original) märzen provide a link between pale lagers and the dark lagers that exist today – throwbacks to the time before Dreher, Sedlmayr and Groll when brown ruled the beer world. These beers include the Bavarian dunkel (dark). This style is now firmly back on the beer lover's radar but it took a brave move by one of Germany's most influential brewers to make this happen. When Prinz Luitpold of Bavaria took control of Kaltenberg, his family's royal brewery, in the mid-1970s, he decided that its fortunes would be best revived by standing out from the crowd rather than competing with it. So, while continuing to produce pale lagers and wheat beers, he decided to also recreate the dunkel style of dark lager that his forebears had once enjoyed and which had faded away during the 20th century. Kaltenberg, in this way, inspired a beer revival that now sees dunkels in production across Germany – beers that are a rich red-brown in colour, with flavours that major on sweet, dark malt notes, such as nut and chocolate, as well as, in some cases, a raisin-like fruitiness.

Also on the way back are dark lagers from elsewhere in Germany and from the Czech Republic. The German schwarzbier (literally, black beer) owes its survival in part to East Germany's Communist regime, where investment in breweries and changes in brewing practice were minimal. Some breweries, unaffected by international commercial pressures, consequently managed to hang onto their smoky, dry dark lagers and these have been enjoyed by the wider world since the fall of the Iron Curtain. Similarly, across the border in the Czech Republic, beers labelled tmavy lezak or cerne (meaning dark lager or black) are also creeping back into the national conscience, having once been prime movers. They tend to be lightly hopped (like other dark lager styles) and have sweetish coffee and cola notes from the malt.

Technicalities

Munich malt is a key ingredient in the production of many dark lagers. It is slightly darker than pilsner malt, because of its higher kilning temperature, but it retains enough viable natural enzymes to convert its own starches into sugars. This means that Munich malt can be used on its own in the mash although, for a dunkel, pilsner malt may also be used. Hops are traditionally German. Vienna lager is still built on a base of Vienna malt which, like Munich malt, has the ability to convert its own starches to sugar while appearing a touch darker than pilsner malt. However, pilsner malt, as well as some darker malts, may be added to recipes. Hops tend to be German or Czech.

For a schwarzbier, a brewer will tend to use mostly Munich malt, along with some pilsner malt and perhaps some well-roasted malts to deepen the colour and add to the toasted flavour, the hops again remaining German. Czech dark lager brewers will typically use pilsner malt and some local darker malts, but may also incorporate Munich malts. The hop regime features Czech Saaz in many cases.

Fermentation for all these beers is with the lager yeast, *Saccharomyces pastorianus*, and, for the best, a long cold maturation period is employed. The final strength tends to fall within the 4.5–5.5% alcohol band, although some Czech dark lagers are weaker.

Visit

Kaltenberg Castle (www.kaltenberg.com), at Geltendorf, some 30 miles west of Munich, is where the dunkel revival began in the 1970s. You can tour the brewery by appointment; otherwise the castle's expansive grounds are open to visitors and you can sup the rich dark König Ludwig Dunkel in the on-site tavern.

For a taste of a dark Czech lager that has never gone away, drop into the famous **U Fleků** pub (ufleku.cz) in Prague where brewing has taken place for possibly 700 years. You won't be the only tourist, so the service can be a bit impersonal at times, but you can at least savour the bar's creamy dark nectar.

Read on

George & Laurie Fix, *Vienna, Märzen, Oktoberfest* (Brewers Publications, 1991)

TASTE OFF!

Dark lagers

Negra Modelo

This amber-red Mexican Vienna combines delicate caramel, light chocolate and warming alcohol with a raisin fruitiness and a firm bitterness, while staying easy to drink because of its clean, slender body. Nutty roasted grains build in the dry finish where raisins and malt linger and a chocolate-like chalkiness develops.

Kaltenberg König Ludwig Dunkel

Hints of treacle and raisin in the aroma lead to a treacle-toffee, initially sweet, taste that is quickly countered by a smack of hops and bitterness from the dark grains. Faint raisin notes hover in the background, with hops emerging more in the drying aftertaste, bringing a herbal finish.

Köstritzer Schwarzbier

Deep garnet in colour, this is a much more bitter beer than the other two, as well-roasted grains really take control, especially in the coffee-like, dry finish after coffee, dark chocolate and hints of liquorice in the smoky taste.

If you want to try more...

... try these other examples:

Vienna: Brooklyn Lager, Eisenbahn 5 Anos, Meantime Union, Samuel Adams Boston Lager, Thornbridge Kill Your Darlings **Dunkel:** Ettaler Kloster Dunkel, Freedom Organic Dark Lager, Hofbräu Dunkel, Weltenburger Kloster Barock Dunkel **Schwarzbier/Czech Dark Lager:** Bernard Dark, Budvar Dark, Eisenbahn Dunkel, Kozel Cerne, Krusovice Cerne

... you may also like:

dubbel, old ale, porter, stout, strong mild

Kaltenberg Castle is where the *dunkel revival* began in the 1970s

Bocks

Bock is a term given to a strong lager. The beer is often pale in colour (and is sometimes labelled heller or helles bock as a result) but, in a throwback to the days when all beers were dark, some bocks are red or deep brown in hue.

The origins of the style lie in the northern German town of Einbeck. Part of the Hanseatic League of merchant cities during the late Middle Ages, the town's speciality was beer (various types of ale) and the quality of its output was renowned. This was a result of strict quality control that operated in Einbeck where there were no private breweries. In order to brew, citizens needed to borrow the public brew kettle, which was delivered to their homes in turn. The beer that resulted was then vetted by town officials before going on sale.

As most of the town's beer was transported some distance, it was made strong, with much of the fermentation still taking place in casks as the beer headed up to the Baltic ports and on to destinations further afield. The beer also made its way south and became exceptionally popular in Bavaria, where, from the turn of the 17th century, the locals learned to produce their own equivalent. With the use of different yeasts and long storage in cold conditions, the fledgling style turned from an ale into a lager. The Bavarians called the beer Einbecker, after its birthplace, but the name – it is said – was soon twisted by the local dialect and then shortened, to end up as bock. Bock also means goat in German, which explains why so many of today's bocks feature a goat on their labels.

Bocks came to be associated with the clergy and many were brewed for consumption in periods of fasting in the run-up to religious festivals such as Christmas, with the rich beer providing monks with energy-giving sugars, vitamins and minerals at a time when solid food was not allowed. At the Munich abbey of the monks of St Francis of Paola the brethren developed a notably fuller, stronger version of bock. They called it Salvator, the Latin for saviour, and it formed part of their Easter rituals, eventually going on sale to the public in 1780. Initial copies by other breweries were also called Salvator, until the title was trademarked by the brewery – now known as Paulaner and no longer run by monks – in 1896. Brewers who produce beers in the same vein today pay homage to the original by adding the suffix 'ator' to the end of their beer's name – as in Celebrator by Ayinger Brewery. Generically, these beers are described as doppelbocks, reflecting the fact that the alcohol content is higher than that found in normal bocks.

Many were brewed for periods of fasting in the run-up to religious festivals such as Christmas

Bocks are now produced all over the world, with Austria, Scandinavia and the Netherlands taking a particular shine to the style and sometimes adding their own twist. The Dutch bokbier comes to the fore in the Netherlands every autumn. It is generally dark in colour and, in some instances, is top-fermented rather than bottom-fermented. The Dutch also produce a paler bock known as Lentebok for spring.

Technicalities

With a strength roughly in the region of 6.5–7% ABV, bock is a naturally malt-accented beer, thanks to the generous quantity of grain required to brew a beer to that strength. The grist is typically composed of lots of pilsner malt, with perhaps a little Munich or Vienna malt to deepen the colour and contribute to the body. Darker versions feature a higher proportion of Munich and/or Vienna and possibly more roasted malts. A soft but full body, and flavours that fall on the sweet side, is the result. Hops are restrained, perhaps offering some lemon or herb notes, and usually drawn from the tried-and-trusted hop gardens of southern Germany. Fermentation is slow, in the bottom-fermenting fashion, with the beer allowed a long and lazy conditioning period which, when combined with the silkiness of the abundant malt, ensures a smooth texture and a mellow flavour. In some doppelbocks (roughly 7% ABV and above), the fruitier qualities of the malt, rather than esters, may shine through.

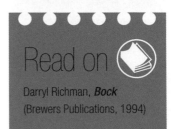

Insight

Another familiar variation on the bock theme (especially in Bavaria) is the maibock. Its name means May bock, and it was conceived to celebrate the start of spring. It is generally pale in colour and differs little from other heller bocks in character.

Read on

Darryl Richman, *Bock* (Brewers Publications, 1994)

Insight 🔍

Not including the weizenbock, which is a type of strong weizen (see the section on Weizens), there is one further member of the bock family. Eisbock is a very strong bock (9% ABV and more) made by freezing the beer after fermentation. The freezing turns some of the liquid (but not the alcohol) into ice, so when the ice is removed the concentration of alcohol is greater.

Visit 🛑

A visit to **Einbeck** (www.einbeck-marketing.de) provides a brewing history lesson. Although there is only one brewery active there today, the prosperity that beer once brought to the city is evident all around. Particularly worthy of note are the wide archways that lead into many of the historic houses. These were the gateways that allowed access for the city's communal brew kettle. Some tourist events are themed around beer, relating the story of the town and the origins of bock.

Winter is the time to visit Bavaria to enjoy bock. The local brewers prepare plenty of warming, malty beers to help fend off the winter chills. As winter draws to a close, there's a final flourish when what is known as **Starkbierzeit** (strong beer time) is celebrated. This is when the season's doppelbocks go on sale. The celebration kicks off on 19 March with an official tapping of the first cask of Salvator at **Paulaner's bierkeller** (www.nockherberg.com) on the top of Munich's highest hill and then runs for two weeks in the city's pubs.

In central Amsterdam, over three days every October, the Dutch consumer group PINT organizes an extremely popular **Bokbierfestival** (www.pint.nl), which provides another excellent reason to visit this bustling city. You can sample dozens of bokbiers from breweries big and small, some regular annual offerings, others one-offs. There's no better way of getting an understanding of the Dutch take on the bock style.

Einbeck's historic houses are evidence of the city's brewing history

TASTE OFF!

Bocks

Hacker-Pschorr Hubertus Bock

A good example of a heller bock, golden in colour. Lemon and lime join aromatic herbs in the slightly bready nose, before a suitably full, smooth and creamy taste, with a little more citrus and a dry, herbal hop bitterness. Sweetness lingers awhile in the otherwise bitter, herbal, thick and grainy finish.

Paulaner Salvator

The classic doppelbock, a russet-coloured beer heavy with raisin, caramel and malt loaf flavours. Smooth, warming and teasingly spicy with alcohol, it's a big, satisfying, tasty brew with a crispness and cleanness indicative of a well-lagered beer.

Van Steenberge Leute Bokbier

A top-fermented interpretation of the Low Countries bock style, this cherryade-red beer comes from a Belgian brewery that specializes in strong ales. It is far leaner and drier than the German bocks, suggesting the use of sugar during brewing. Stewed apple, raisins and faint chocolate layer the bittersweet taste, before a bitter finish.

If you want to try more...

... try these other examples:

Bock: Andechs Bergbock Hell, Ayinger Maibock, Einbecker Ur-Bock, Weltenburger Kloster Asam Bock **Doppelbock:** Augustiner Maximator, Ayinger Celebrator, Eggenberger Urbock 23°, Kaltenberg Ritterbock, Löwenbräu Triumphator **Dutch bok:** Amstel Bock, Christoffel Bok, 't IJ Ijbok, Jopen 4-Granen Bok, Texels Bock

... you may also like:

barley wine, dubbel, dunkel, helles, weizenbock

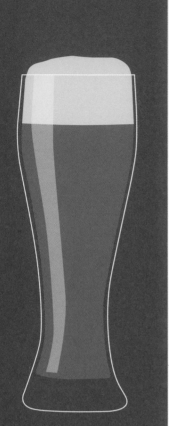

Weizens

Weizen is a German wheat beer style, also commonly known as weissbier, meaning white beer, although the beer is mostly yellow-orange in colour. Its origins lie in Bavaria, in the south of the country, where its production was controlled by the royal family for almost 200 years. Only in 1872 were common brewers finally allowed to produce the beer. Some say this monopoly was kept in place to enable the aristocracy to enjoy the finer qualities of wheat in beer, leaving coarser barley beer for the masses, or to keep wheat prices low for bread production, but it is more likely that controlling supply was simply a very handsome money-spinner for the monarchy at a time when pale wheat beers were more popular than brown barley beers. During the 20th century weizen consumption fell away but the style gained a new lease of life from the 1960s when younger drinkers began to appreciate its accessible flavours and easy drinkability.

The weizen is universally known for its extravagant fruit and spice notes, all of which are derived purely from the natural beer ingredients: there are no added spices or fruits – this is against the rule of the Reinheitsgebot, the German beer purity law, which permits only barley, wheat, water, hops and yeast in the making of beer. These astonishing flavours come instead from the action of the yeast during fermentation. The beer is warm-fermented, which means it is liable to develop more fruit flavours than a cold-fermented beer in the first place, but the selection of yeast strain is significant. Brewers employ a special wheat beer yeast that really goes to town in creating fruit and spice flavours, typically apple, banana, clove and vanilla.

The finished beer – usually in the region of 5–5.5% ABV – has a high carbonation, which develops a deep, rocky head of foam when poured into its traditional vase-like glass. It is also usually served cloudy, with yeast and proteins left in suspension, and is a very distinctive sight in Germany's summer biergartens. Outside Germany, in some cases, the beer is served with a slice of lemon but this is discouraged by purists.

As beer styles have begun to wander the world so new slants on weizen have been developed. Weizens from the US, the UK or other countries may be rather different in character. They may look similar but may have a more pronounced bitterness or citrus character, because of the different hops and yeasts used. The compliment has now been passed back to Germany, where some brewers, including wheat specialist Schneider, are becoming more adventurous with their wheat beers.

Weizen is universally known for its extravagant fruit and spice notes

Darker versions of weizens are known as dunkelweizens or dunkelweiss. These are produced in the same way but the grist includes a percentage of dark grains, giving the beer a deeper colour and offering roasted malt flavours such as caramel and chocolate. Strong versions of weizens are called weizenbocks – wheat beer at a bock strength. Typically, these range in strength from 7% to 8.5% ABV, and pack in even more of the complex fruit and spices notes found in weizen.

Technicalities

Weizen is not produced using only wheat. Instead, a blend of barley malt and malted wheat is used as natural enzymes in the barley are needed to help convert the starches in the wheat into fermentable sugars and the husks of the barley are required to act as a natural filter during the run-off from mashing. However, there is usually a very high percentage of wheat (50% minimum, by law in Germany) in the mix. For dunkelweizen, and some weizenbocks, Munich or Vienna malt is often added, but some of the dark colour and flavour may also come from roasted wheat malt. Hops provide a modest balancing bitterness and, of course, some natural preservative qualities, but are generally second-fiddle ingredients in these styles of beer. Typical hop varieties used are local German ones, such as Hallertauer Tradition, Magnum or Hersbrucker. In place of pronounced hop character in the taste, the brewer aims to showcase the wonders of the yeast, which is a special strain called *Torulaspora delbrueckii* that is related to the *Saccharomyces cerevisiae* used for other ales.

Weizen is traditionally decoction-mashed, but improvements in malt quality mean that many breweries now employ infusion, temperature-controlled mashing, with a number of rests taking place during the process, to prevent the mash becoming too thick and to help deconstruct the proteins. Ferulic acid develops during a rest held at around 45°C (113°F). This is important as it later works with the yeast to develop a phenol (a weak acid) known as 4-vinyl guaiacol, which gives the beer its familiar clove flavours. Fermentation is often in open fermenters, which are considered to help boost the production of such phenols and also esters such as isoamyl acetate, which is responsible for weizen's distinctive banana notes.

Read on

Stan Hieronymus, *Brewing with Wheat* (Brewers Publications, 2010)

Visit

Bavaria is the place to visit to really understand the popularity and culture of weizen. Make plans to enjoy a glass in one of the huge biergartens in Munich, where you can sip your beer in the shade of a horse chestnut tree, and then drop into the **Weisses Brauhaus** (www.weisses-brauhaus. de), close to the famous Marienplatz. This was the original Schneider brewery and it's now a big, bustling tavern where you can enjoy the full, extensive range of the company's weizens, several of them on draught. Further north, at Kelheim on the River Danube, you can tour the current **Schneider brewery** (www.schneider-weisse.de) at 2pm on Tuesdays (plus the same time on Thursdays, April–October). As they only brew weizen there, you'll learn rather a lot about this style.

Weisses Brauhaus serves the full range of Schneider's weizens

TASTE OFF!

Weizens

Franziskaner Weissbier

Hazy yellow in colour, with all that you would expect from the style in the bready, slightly savoury aroma – vanilla, banana, clove and bubblegum – this is a straight-down-the-middle weizen with the same flavours repeated in the taste, while clove bitterness builds in the cracker-like finish.

Weihenstephaner Hefeweissbier Dunkel

Gentle roasted grain notes run through this dark amber beer. Caramel joins typical weizen flavours such as banana, vanilla, bubblegum, a hint of clove and a little stewed apple in the aroma and taste. There's more caramel in the smooth, dry, softly bitter finish.

Schneider Aventinus

A hazy chestnut colour, this weizenbock is a much bolder beer than the first two and is loaded with fruit and spice flavours. Apples, cloves, banana and marzipan are the main features in the bittersweet taste, with more bitterness developing in the dry finish, where banana and clove linger. It's complex but remarkably light for the strength (8.2% ABV).

If you want to try more...

... try these other examples:

Weizen: Baltika No. 8 Wheat, Erdinger Weissbier, Kaltenberg König Ludwig Weissbier Hell, Maisel's Weisse, Meantime Wheat, Schneider Weisse, Thornbridge Versa **Dunkelweizen:** Franziskaner Dunkel Hefe-Weisse, Kaltenberg König Ludwig Weissbier Dunkel **Weizenbock:** Eisenbahn Weizenbock, Erdinger Pikantus, Weihenstephaner Vitus

... you may also like:

witbier

Hops in witbier are chosen for their preservative qualities, leaving the door open for spices to create their own character

Other wheat beers

Just as the good folk of Bavaria have enjoyed beers made with wheat for centuries, so have drinkers in other parts of the world. The products they have created, however, are notably different from the richly phenolic and fruity beers of southern Germany.

Witbier

The best-known wheat beer style beyond weizen is the Belgian witbier (also known in French as bière blanche). Like its German cousin, it too has come back from obscurity. Indeed, the witbier was virtually dead as a beer style until it was revived, with huge success, in the 1960s. The man responsible was Pierre Celis, a dairyman who lamented the absence of the white beers he used to drink in his homeland to the east of Brussels. These were beers that dated back centuries and were brewed with wheat grown locally and then flavoured with exotic spices shipped in from the Far East and the Caribbean by Dutch sailors. The spices were probably required to mask the taste because, in those days, beer turned sour quickly. Archives recall historic samples being rather lactic, with a sour milk note.

Celis, who had worked for a while at a brewery where witbiers were produced, decided to start his own business. The white beer he created he called Hoegaarden, after the town in which his brewery was situated. It rapidly attracted the attention not just of local drinkers but of beer fans across Belgium. Celis's business was eventually sold to the company that is now known as A-B InBev, one of the world's giant breweries, and Hoegaarden is internationally available. It remains the best known of the witbier-style beers but there are also many, arguably better, others now in production.

Although the beer's name translates as white beer, the beer is usually a pale yellow colour, but with a chalky sheen from the yeast and proteins that have been left in suspension. The best witbiers are bottle conditioned, but some are pasteurized, so the presence of yeast in the bottle does not guarantee a bottle-fermented beer. Flavourwise, the wheat in the beer creates a gentle tartness and a subtle cereal note that does not detract from the spices that are added. The most common spices are ground coriander and dried, bitter orange peel, but you may also discover beers including other ingredients. They are generally added to the beer during the copper boil, offering a fragrant citrus and pepper note. The strength is around 5% ABV.

Berliner weisse

Somewhat different in taste is another type of wheat beer, this time from Berlin. The Berliner weisse is a spritzy, low-alcohol (around 3% ABV) sour beer, made by allowing *Lactobacillus* bacteria to strut its stuff. This induces a tart acidic note to the beer, which is often mitigated by drinkers in bars asking for a dash of raspberry- or woodruff-based (red or green) syrup to be added. Just one major brewery maintains this beer style in its native Berlin (Kindl), and that is only in bottles, but smaller breweries locally and further afield have begun reviving it.

Gose

Related to the Berliner weisse is gose, a beer style that was forgotten by most drinkers until very recently. It is still only rarely found, in versions brewed by adventurous breweries who have raided archives for recipes, but its distinctive ingredient is a dosing of salt.

Technicalities

Witbier is made using a good proportion of wheat (generally around 30–50%) alongside barley malt. Sometimes oats are added, too, for creaminess. Unlike for German weizen, the wheat is not malted. This is probably a throwback to the time when such beers were brewed by farmers, who simply opted for the cheaper, raw wheat option. The downside of using unmalted wheat is that, while the wheat's starch can be accessed by cracking the grain, there are few natural enzymes to convert it to sugar – hence the inclusion of barley in the grist and usually the need for a long rest period during mashing to allow the barley's enzymes to do their work. Hops in witbier are chosen for their preservative qualities and gentle balancing bitterness rather than flavour, leaving the door open for spices to create their own character, although some historians claim the spiciness of modern examples is far less subtle than in the more restrained beers of previous centuries. The yeast used is a top-fermenting ale yeast (*Saccharomyces cerevisiae*).

Berliner weisse is an even more complicated beast. Historically, its sour notes were generated when *Lactobacillus* bacteria naturally invaded the beer. This was possible for a number of reasons, not least the fact that the wort – consisting of malted (not unmalted) wheat and barley – often remained unboiled, giving free rein to infections and not allowing natural preservatives in the hops to be infused. Techniques today may involve separating the wort into two batches and fermenting one with ale yeast and the other (unboiled) with *Lactobacillus*, before finally blending the two to achieve the desired level of acidity.

Insight

Another forgotten wheat beer style is also making a comeback. *Grodziskie* is a low-alcohol beer of Polish origin made from a grist composed entirely of smoked wheat malt. It is otherwise known as Grätzer, a name it acquired through the 19th-century Prussian occupation of Poland.

Read on

Stan Hieronymus, **Brewing with Wheat** (Brewers Publications, 2010)

Gose remains a rarity. Its origins lie in the town of Goslar, near Leipzig, but it shares attributes with wheat beers from other parts of Europe. For a start, its grist of malted wheat and barley may originally have been spontaneously fermented by wild yeasts, like a lambic from Belgium (see Lambics). Secondly, it also featured the work of *Lactobacillus*, as in Berliner weisse. Thirdly, as well as salt, the beer was seasoned with coriander, as in Belgian witbier (in a rare derogation from the German beer purity law because the style of beer predated it). Because all production of the style ceased during the 20th century, it is difficult to assess whether today's interpretations are true to the original, but the beer makes an interesting diversion in any wheat beer discussion.

Visit

The **Hoegaarden brewery** (hoegaarden.com) in the town of the same name is open for tours and the Kouterhof restaurant/bar on site makes a good refreshment stop afterwards, with its atmospheric vaulted brick ceiling. The importance of witbier to the area is demonstrated as you enter the town, with an old brew kettle now adorning one of the traffic roundabouts.

To understand the culture of Berliner weisse, and in particular the use of syrups to mask the sourness, the only place to visit is Berlin itself and, within Berlin, the prime location is the **Alt Berliner Weissbierstube** (www.alt-berliner-weissbierstube.de). You can also take the **Kindl-Schultheiss brewery** tour (www.schultheiss.de), but the emphasis is more on other beers rather than Berliner weisse.

For an insight into gose, probably the best place to visit is the historic **Ohne Bedenken bar** (www.gosenschenke.de) in Leipzig, where owner Lothar Goldhahn has made strenuous efforts to breathe new life into this foundering style.

TASTE OFF!

Other wheat beers

Caracole Troublette

A more interesting example of a witbier than the omnipresent Hoegaarden, this is a typically slightly hazy, golden beer with aromas of bread, sherbet lemons, peppery coriander and hints of bubblegum. Sweet bready cereals support flavours of bitter earthy spices, the lemon and orange notes of coriander and a peppery warmth, before a peppery, earthy-spicy, bitter finish.

Berliner Kindl Weisse

Attractively pale yellow, this is a deceptive and uncompromising beer with a lemon aroma. The taste is screw-up-your face tart, just like squeezing unsweetened lemon juice on the tongue, but also spritzy. The acidity can be felt on the teeth in the very dry, tart lemon finish. Highly refreshing, but it's easy to see why the Germans drink it with a shot of syrup.

Bayerischer Bahnhof Original Leipziger Gose

They aim to add just enough sea salt to this beer so that it doesn't quite reach the human taste threshold, but there's a definite salty sensation, if not a pronounced salty taste, to this hazy, easy-drinking golden beer. Flavours otherwise fall just on the sweet side, with a light tartness and acidity from the work of the *Lactobacillus* bacteria and an orange and softly peppery note from the coriander.

If you want to try more…

… try these other examples:
Witbier: Du Bocq Blanche de Namur, Hitachino Nest White Ale, Hoegaarden, La Trappe Witte, Lefèbvre Blanche de Bruxelles, Van Eecke Watou's Wit **Berliner weisse:** 1809 Berliner Weisse Style, Hawkshead Solar Sour, The Kernel London Sour **Gose:** Döllnitzer Ritterguts Gose, St Austell Steady as She Gose, Samuel Adams Verloren Gose

… you may also like:
Witbier: weizen **Berliner weisse:** Flemish red, gueuze, lambic, oud bruin **Gose:** gueuze, weizen

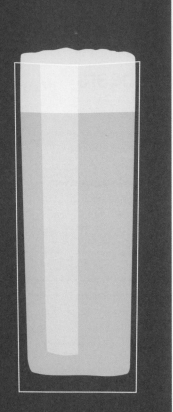

Regional German styles

Contrary to many people's impressions, Germany is not just a lager and wheat beer country. True, hell, pils, bock and weizen dominate the country's output and consumption, but other historic beer styles still survive in the regions.

Kölsch

The best-known of these styles is kölsch. As its name suggests, it is a style indigenous to the city of Cologne (Köln in German), created, it is said, as a response to the rapid spread of golden pilsner at the end of the 19th century. Ask for a beer in the city's pubs and restaurants and this is what you will be served. While there are around 10 breweries producing kölsch, each with their own subtle interpretation of the style, the broad characteristics, set down since 1986 in a convention that protects the beer, are a pale, bright appearance, a top fermentation and an obvious hop presence. To this, brewers have traditionally added a period of cold conditioning, making kölsch a sort of ale/lager hybrid.

Kölsch is a very delicate beer, with a soft fruity or floral flavour from the hops and a spritzy crispness that makes it very moreish. It is one of the most subtle of beer styles and therefore doesn't stand up to bottling particularly well. For a true kölsch experience you really have to drink the beer fresh, served by a fastidious waiter (known as a kobe) who plonks a small glass (a stange) down on your table as he races through the pub.

Altbier

Cologne's northern neighbour, Düsseldorf, is home to another idiosyncratic beer style. This is called alt, or altbier. The name means old and refers to the top-fermented style of brewing in use before bottom-fermented lagers came on the scene. Alt is a darker beer than kölsch, resembling more a British bitter or a Belgian pale ale in its shades of copper and brown. Hops are more pronounced than in kölsch but, like kölsch, the beer undergoes a long cold-conditioning period. The result is a beer with notes of caramel and nut from the malt, a firm and often floral hop character and the clean crispness of a lager. Variations on the theme may be found from breweries in other parts of northern Germany.

Germany is not just a lager and wheat beer country

Rauchbier

The other notable maverick German beer style is the rauchbier. A speciality of the Franconia region of northern Bavaria, and in particular the World Heritage city of Bamberg, this is a beer made with a good proportion of smoked malt. The beer is usually a strong lager, but weizen versions also exist and all are characterized by a pronounced smoky aroma and flavour, offering suggestions of bonfires, kippers and bacon. It is an acquired taste but some versions are very accessible and you can soon find yourself won over.

Technicalities

Kölsch is made from pilsner malt and traditional German hops such as Hersbrucker and Tettnanger but there is one other key ingredient and that is provenance. Only beers produced in the Cologne metropolitan area are entitled to be called kölsch as the beer has European Union PGI (Protected Geographical Indication) status and is also policed by the local brewing convention. Beers from elsewhere in Germany (and indeed the wider world) that otherwise follow the style guidelines cannot be called kölsch and are therefore labelled 'Cologne-style beer' or similar. Fermented with an ale yeast, sometimes at a slightly lower temperature than for other ales, kölsch rolls out at around 4.8% ABV.

Altbier is commonly produced using pilsner malt along with Munich and/or Vienna malt. The hops, again, are mild-mannered old German favourites such as Spalt, but they provide a good level of bitterness in this style of beer. Fermentation, with an ale yeast, takes place somewhere between the temperatures needed for lager and ale, roughly in the area of 15–19°C (59–66°F), which leads to fewer esters than in other top-fermenting beers. The end product features between 4.5% and 4.8% ABV.

Rauchbier is typically made like a lager (the most famous example, Schlenkerla, is actually a märzen at heart), with a strength of around 5–6% ABV. The big difference is in the use of smoked malt. In Franconia, this malt is dried over beechwood. Care must be taken to ensure that phenolic notes derived from the smokiness of the malt do not swamp the beer and make it taste too medicinal. The growing appreciation of rauchbier has led brewers in other parts of the world to experiment with smoked malt, creating smoked porters and other delights.

Read on

John Conen, *Bamberg & Franconia: A Guide to Beers, Breweries & Pubs* (John Conen, 2010)

Geoff Larson and Ray Daniels, *Smoked Beers: History, Brewing Techniques, Recipes* (Brewers Publications, 2001)

Eric Warner, *Kölsch: History, Brewing Techniques, Recipes* (Brewers Publications, 1998)

Visit

To try both kölsch and alt at their very best, you must visit their home cities. In Cologne, be prepared to be served only small glasses of the local brew. Initially, you'll feel short changed but, as the beers keep on coming, you'll appreciate the locals' measured way of drinking. Observing the waiters dashing around the tables with their swaying trays of glasses is entertainment in itself, but the chance to wander the city, visiting bars run by different breweries and sampling their respective kölsches, is the real

pleasure of a visit. You can start in the massive **Früh** (www.frueh.de) and **Gaffel** (www.gaffelamdom.de) pubs near the station and cathedral and then wander off into the Old Town to find smaller, more homely establishments.

Düsseldorf offers similar delights and four brewpubs in particular – **Zum Uerige** (www.uerige.de), **Zum Schlüssel** (www.zumschluessel.de), **Schumacher** (www.schumacher-alt. de) and **Im Füchschen**

(fuechschen.de) – are essential visits. As in Cologne, the beer may be tapped fresh from a cask and served in small glasses.

The primary place to visit to see rauchbier appreciated on its home turf is the **Schlenkerla** pub (www. schlenkerla.de) in Bamberg. Then you can meander through the streets to visit one of the other 10 breweries in the centre, including **Spezial** (www.brauerei-spezial.de), another rauchbier specialist.

Kölsch is best appreciated in pubs such as *Cologne's Gaffel am Dom*

TASTE OFF!

Regional German styles

Gaffel Kölsch

Typically golden in colour, this is one of the best-known examples of kölsch. Note the sweet cereals, lemon and floral notes in the aroma that carry on into the mostly sweet, crisp and spritzy taste, where a mild herbal note joins them, continuing into the drying, increasingly bitter finish.

Schlösser Alt

The rich chestnut colour suggests a beer with a full malt character and that's also evident in the aroma where a bready note is topped by caramel and hazelnut. The taste is bittersweet, with more nut and caramel, plus a hint of tea, but there's not too much body. Bitterness develops in the dry, nutty finish.

Heller-Trum Aecht Schlenkerla Rauchbier Märzen

This ruby-coloured beer is all about the smoke, from the pronounced bonfire and smoky bacon crisps aroma to the smoky, dry, slowly bitter finish. In-between, the taste falls just on the bitter side, with a meaty, woody, bonfire flavour and yet only a slender body.

If you want to try more...

... try these other examples:
Kölsch: Früh Kölsch, Küppers Kölsch, Thornbridge Tzara **Alt:** Diebels Alt, Duckstein, Samuel Adams Boston Ale, Zum Uerige Alt **Rauchbier:** Heller-Trum Aecht Schlenkerla Rauchweizen, Spezial Rauchbier Märzen

... you may also like:
Kölsch: golden ale, helles, märzen, pilsner **Alt:** Belgian pale ale, bitter, India pale ale **Rauchbier:** other smoked beers

Saisons & bières de garde

Saison and bière de garde are not so much beer styles as traditions. The origins of both lie on the farm: in the case of the former, farms in the French-speaking Wallonia region of Belgium and, in the case of the latter, farms just across the border in France. In character, the beers seem rather different but they share a heritage that dates back to the time when brewing in summer was impossible because of the ambient temperature and the wild yeasts and bacteria that filled the warm air. Farmers would brew beer up until springtime and then serve it to their workers through the summer months, or perhaps keep some back for a celebration at harvest time when, with fresh barley and hops in store and the temperature falling, brewing could begin again.

This does not, of course, offer any clue as to the type of beer being produced. It is likely that such seasonal beer (hence the term saison, from the French) for summer consumption would have been a quenching, restorative brew, ideal for refreshing the labourers on the land. For the celebration, maybe something more substantial was tucked away. And it is this vagueness that gives rise to the situation today in which Belgian saisons often have little in common with each other, let alone with their French neighbour.

From the success of Saison Dupont – the star of a family business near the city of Tournai – the implication is that saison is a spritzy, well-carbonated pale beer, with citrus hop character and a searingly dry, spicy finish. But if you take the saison from the Silly brewery (named after a village just north of Mons), you'll find it darker in colour and much sweeter. Other Belgian breweries play around in the gap between the two.

Today's bières de garde, on the other hand, provide a better link to the bigger, richer beers that were perhaps held back for harvest celebrations. There is a clue in the name: bière de garde means beer for keeping – generally several weeks at the brewery after fermentation although, in the past, maturation probably lasted months. These are chunkier, sweeter, maltier beers than saisons and derive a mild spicy note from the selection of hops. If we take Jenlain Ambrée from Duyck brewery, near Valenciennes, as the benchmark of the style, we can assume that bière de garde is a deep amber beer, with around 7.5% ABV and a bittersweet taste of delicate herbs and spices. On the other hand, a beer such as Ch'ti Blonde from the Castelain brewery, near Lens, is golden and sweet. From this it is clear that, with both saison and bière de garde – neither of which is brewed only seasonally these days – we can only talk in vague generalities.

Technicalities

A typical saison today offers around 5–8% ABV, with most at the lower end of that spectrum. Saison Dupont – the template used by many brewers around the world – is produced using pilsner malt and Golding hops. The hardness of the water in the region contributes to the dryness of the beer, and bottle-conditioning – at least six weeks at the brewery before release – produces a healthy, natural effervescence to add to the quenching character. Dupont and other saisons, from the action of the top-fermenting yeast, have an inherent spiciness and notable fruit notes. Some brewers, however, also add spices such as coriander, black pepper and orange peel to emphasize the difference between a saison and a simple pale ale.

A typical bière de garde falls roughly into the 6–8.5% ABV bracket. Jenlain Ambrée features pale and roasted malts in the grist, the latter adding notes of caramel and nut to counter the tangy, herbal flavours derived from French-grown Strisselspalt, Magnum and Brewers Gold hops. Jenlain also has a Blonde equivalent, acknowledging that golden is acceptable for a bière de garde. Like saisons, bières de garde are top-fermented, ale-type beers although fermentation temperatures are kept low in order to avoid excessive ester creation. Most bières de garde are not bottle conditioned. They have done their maturing at the brewery before going on sale.

Read on

Phil Markowski, *Farmhouse Ales: Culture and Craftsmanship in the Belgian Tradition* (Brewers Publications, 2004)

Arthur Taylor, *Good Beer Guide to Northern France* (CAMRA Books, 1998)

Visit

Tours are available all year round at **St Feuillien** (www.st-feuillien.com), just north-east of Mons, which produces a saison). At the end of September every year, **Dupont** (www.brasserie-dupont.com) opens its doors to the public, offering free guided tours as part of the Tourpes en Activité weekend. Not far away, **La Brasserie à Vapeur** (www.vapeur.com), near Tournai, is open for guided tours most Sunday mornings and you can also watch them brewing on the last Saturday of the month. In France, the **Castelain brewery** (www.chti.com), which brews Ch'ti beers, is open for self-guided tours every day, except Sunday. **La Choulette brewery** (www.lachoulette.com) at Hordain, near Valenciennes, has an open weekend every November to celebrate the launch of its Bière de Noël.

TASTE OFF!

Saisons & bières de garde

Saison Dupont

For many brewers, this is the archetypal saison. It's a lean, notably dry and mostly bitter beer, with plenty of lively carbonation. The flavours combine bitter citrus fruit, hints of pineapple and typically perfumed Belgian yeast notes, along with a spicy, peppery warmth.

Duyck Jenlain Ambrée

Toasted malt not only colours this beer a rich amber, but also delivers caramel notes in the sweet, full taste. These are offset by liquorice-like herbal flavours that run on into the drying, bittersweet finish. A big, smooth beer.

Castelain Ch'ti Blonde

Exemplifying the golden style of bière de garde, this beer has very little in common with Jenlain Ambrée and other darker variants of the style, apart from a mild herbal note in the taste and finish. Otherwise, it showcases a honey-like sweetness and a peppery coriander-like spiciness that nods towards the Belgian saison.

If you want to try more…

… try these other examples:
Saison: St Feuillien Saison, Silly Saison, Vapeur Saison de Pipaix
Bière de garde: La Choulette Ambrée, St-Sylvestre Trois Monts, Thornbridge Jehanne

… you may also like:
Belgian blond ale, India pale ale, pale ale, strong ale, tripel, witbier

Rochefort is one of only 11 Trappist monasteries brewing *Trappist* beer

Trappist & abbey beers

The designations Trappist and abbey refer not to a style of beer but its origins. For many centuries, religious settlements brewed their own beers, sometimes just for their own consumption but at other times also for the local community. Beer ensured the monks and their guests had something safe to drink when local water supplies were infected and also provided nourishment in liquid form during times of fasting. But many monasteries were secularized or closed when wars raged across Europe and, with the arrival of commercial breweries, most of the surviving, or re-opened, monastic orders relinquished their own production. There are still several that brew – most in Belgium – although some are monasteries that have come back into the business fairly recently, having recognized the potential revenue that beer offers.

The majority of the monasteries and abbeys that brew belong to the Trappist brotherhood, a division of the Benedictine order. Only beers produced at these monasteries can officially be labelled Trappist, and then only as long as the beer is brewed within the monastery; production (even if done by outside workers) is at least supervised by the fraternity; brewing remains a secondary activity; and all profits go only towards the upkeep of the abbey or good causes. Breweries that do not conform to these rules can only call their products abbey beers. Some of these work on behalf of, or remit funds to, active religious settlements; others simply cash-in on the idea by using names of saints and defunct abbeys.

That said, there are many similarities between Trappist and abbey beers. On both sides, a brewery's range can begin with a beer around 4.5–7% ABV, historically known as a singel or enkel and often blond in colour (see also Golden ales). Traditionally, this was a weaker beer designed for everyday consumption by the monks themselves, but now such beers are increasingly finding their way into the wider world, the most common being Chimay Gold. Then there is a dubbel, which is a strong, vinous brown ale with about 6.5–8% ABV. The name means double but clearly the beer is not double the strength of a singel. The same applies to tripel, which is not three times as strong, rolling out at around 8–10% ABV. This is a golden beer, with lots of fruity esters and also a firm hop character. A further level, increasingly known as quadrupel or abt (meaning abbot), and comprising aromatic brown beers, takes the alcohol range over 10% ABV.

Only beers produced at these monasteries can officially be labelled Trappist

Technicalities

Strength is a prominent feature of Trappist and abbey beers, but what is remarkable about most examples is that they are not thick or cloying. The reason for this is that brewers use sugar in many brews. This gives the yeast plenty to chew on and results in alcohol generation without the rich flavours and body that the use of malt alone to provide that much sugar would bring. It means the beers are strong, but still relatively slender, with a moreish dryness.

The main base malt for many Trappist and abbey beers is pilsner malt. In darker beers, such as dubbels and quadrupels, some dark malts may be used, supplemented by dark candi sugar – added during the copper boil – which helps deepen the colour and contributes notes of caramel and raisins. Hops, across the range, are generally Old World types, such as Saaz and Savinjsky Goldings. Carbonation is commonly elevated, especially in tripels, helping to keep the beer spritzy and refreshing, despite the daunting strength. The type of yeast used – a top-fermenting ale strain – is crucial to the character of all these beers. It not only must cope well with the alcohol it generates but also needs to develop esters. This is aided by brewers maintaining a high fermentation temperature.

After fermentation, nearly all Trappist beers and many abbey beers are bottle conditioned, with further maturation in the being bottle a key part of the brewing process. Pick up a bottle and you'll often see the best before date set several years into the future. As these beers age, hop character declines but fruitiness develops, with oxidation slowly adding notes of Madeira and port wine to the darker beers. Some specialist bars and shops offer a choice of young or aged beer. Take your pick. This idea is particularly relevant for Orval. The one beer sold commercially by this abbey is bottled with some *Brettanomyces* yeast, which develops its dry, spicy flavours over time and young examples may not show much evidence of its effect.

Insight

Beers from the Rochefort (6, 8 and 10) and Westvleteren (8 and 12) breweries are known primarily by numbers, rather than names. These numbers are historic, reflecting the original gravity of the beer as calculated using a now obsolete measuring system known as Belgian degrees.

Read on

Stan Hieronymus, *Brew Like a Monk* (Brewers Publications, 2005)

Michael Jackson, *Great Beers of Belgium* (Brewers Publications, 2008)

Roger Protz, *Heavenly Beer* (Carroll and Brown, 2010)

The International Trappist Association (www.trappist.be)

Insight

There are currently 11 breweries allowed to use the Trappist label. Six of these are in Belgium – Achel, Chimay, Orval, Rochefort, Westmalle and Westvleteren – and two are in the Netherlands – the long established La Trappe, and Zundert, opened at Abdij Maria Toevlucht, near Breda in 2013. These have been joined in recent years by Stift Engelszell in Austria, Spencer (St Joseph's) in Massachusetts, in the US, and Tre Fontane, in Rome. A monastery in France, Abbaye Mont des Cats, also markets a Trappist beer, but this is brewed for it by Chimay.

Visit

Access to Trappist breweries is very limited. While entrance to monastery grounds can be quite liberal, most of the brotherhoods do not allow the public to enter their brewhouses, except perhaps on special occasions. **Orval** (www.orval.be), for example, opens up for one weekend a year, usually in mid-September. An exception is **Koningshoeven** (www.koningshoeven. nl), better known as La Trappe, near Tilburg in the Netherlands, where tours can be enjoyed at weekends (and also during weekdays in summer). That said, most of the others have a café attached or close by where you can sample the beers and perhaps watch a film about their production. At **Achel** (www. achelsekluis.org), you can even see into the brewery from the café.

The *brewery at Orval* is open to visitors once a year, in September

TASTE OFF!

Trappist & abbey beers

La Trappe Dubbel

As dubbels go, La Trappe's is a relatively simple beer. Amber-red in colour, it presents an initial aroma of caramel and vanilla with emerging suggestions of orange and bubblegum. The taste is not as vinous as in other examples of the style, but rather mellow, sweet and creamy, with notes of bubblegum, spice, raisins and oranges. Soft caramel lingers in the creamy, drying, bittersweet finish that has a slightly woody hop note.

Westmalle Tripel

Considered the benchmark of the tripel style, this is a bright yellow-golden beer that packs a mighty punch. After an aroma that is lemony, spicy, bready and piney, alcohol zips across the palate, bringing lots of peppery, perfumed floral notes, offset by gentle lemon and tangy, piney hops. Plenty of carbonation helps achieve crispness, despite the weight of alcohol. Bitterness builds in the warming, peppery finish as tangy, pithy, piney hops linger on and on.

Rochefort 10

A masterclass in strong beer, this red-amber ale skilfully combines complex fruit and spice with a surprising delicateness. Strawberry ice lollies, vanilla, pears and a hint of toffee feature in the aroma, with strawberries, vanilla and peppery spice leading the way in the taste. There are hints of almond and aniseed, a little caramel and raisin from the malt and a squeeze of lemon from the added coriander that, thankfully, doesn't swamp the palate. For such a strong beer, the finish is notably dry, leaving a moderate bitterness, some woody hop notes, more aniseed-like spiciness and a faint nuttiness.

If you want to try more...

... try these other examples:
Dubbel: Ampleforth Abbey Beer Dubbel, Chimay Rouge, Westmalle Dubbel **Tripel:** Chimay White, Maredsous 10, St Bernardus Tripel **Quadrupel:** La Trappe Quadrupel, St Bernardus Abt 12, Westvleteren Abt

... you may also like:
barley wine, bock, old ale, strong mild

Oud Beersel keeps alive the skills of *lambic* blending

Lambics

It is easily assumed that the beer world simply splits neatly into two parts – top-fermented ale and bottom-fermented lager – but there is actually a third method of fermentation that plays a small but increasingly important role in brewing. This involves beer that is spontaneously fermented by wild yeasts in the atmosphere.

In beer's early years, wild yeast fermentation would have been how all beer was created. The first brewers had no idea what it was that caused their soaked grains to foam or what made the liquid taste so much better. Yeast was a great unknown. In time, as we have seen, brewers began to harvest ale and lager yeasts and to use them to their best potential but, in some small corners of the world – most notably in an area just to the west of Brussels – certain brewers still resist innovation and continue to place their faith in the natural world. The end result somehow manages to blur the distinction between beer and wine.

The area of Belgium known as Payottenland is home today to a scattering of breweries. Their output is specialist. They produce a beer style called lambic, the name possibly derived from the town of Lembeek in the region. To produce this beer, the brewers rely on wild yeasts in the atmosphere. They begin with a grist not dissimilar to that of a Belgian witbier, with a high proportion of unmalted wheat. The choice, of course, is deliberate: the brewers are looking for a very light cereal base upon which the unusual flavours created by the wild yeasts can be showcased. Similarly, hop flavours are very restrained. Their preservative qualities are needed as this type of beer is aged for many months before going on sale, but their flavours are not, hence the use of rather old and stale hops that have been hanging around for two or three years since harvest. These are hops that any other brewer would not touch with a bargepole. They are tired and cheesy, with little to commend them, but this means the lambic brewer can use them in great quantity – perhaps five or six times as many as another brewer would use – and thus maximize their preservative qualities. After a long boil (possibly three hours), the beer is cooled not by modern-day methods but by being pumped into a large, shallow tray called a coolship that is open to the elements. It resides at the top of the brewery where shutters are opened overnight to allow in the outside air. This not only cools the wort but also brings in wild yeasts and other (friendly) bacteria that settle into the liquid. Once cool, the wort is run into large wooden casks. Here, the wild yeasts begin their work, creating alcohol while the bacteria develop acidity.

In beer's early years, wild yeast fermentation would have been how all beer was created

After several months, if not a few years, the beer is tapped and blended with the contents of other casks. This is a work of great skill, based on years of tasting experience. The blenders really know how to balance the flavours. The resulting product is known as plain lambic. Some is served young. It is a sharp, cidery drink, tart and fruity but often flat, as carbonation has escaped through the wood during fermentation. As lambic ages, it becomes more sherry-like. Comparisons have been drawn with fino sherry, which shares lambic's dry tartness and is also fermented using wild yeasts. Aged lambic can also be blended with a younger, more lively lambic for bottle-conditioning, creating – after several months in bottle at the brewery – an effervescent, sour and acidic beer that is called gueuze and often likened to Champagne. Some lambic is also sweetened and goes on sale under the name faro but, having once been exceptionally popular, this is increasingly rare. Lambic may also be given a further fermentation with fruit in wooden casks or metal tanks. The fruit not only adds flavour but also provides fresh sugars for the yeast to work on. The most popular fruit used is cherry, with the finished beer known as kriek, although raspberry (making framboise/frambozen in French/Flemish) is also popular and other fruits are also used. The most commercial of these fruit beers are almost like alcopops, being sweet and overly fruity; others are extremely elegant and restrained, the fruit just adding a blush of colour and a soft fruitiness to an otherwise assertive lambic.

Although Payottenland remains the home of lambic production, many brewers around the world are now experimenting with wild yeast beers. Some of these are fermented by yeasts in their local environment and others by yeasts

Elgood's **brewery uses its cooling trays to brew** *lambic-style* **beer**

that have been deliberately added for this effect, although none is eligible to use the name lambic. In the UK, Elgood's brewery in Wisbech has dusted off its long-retired cooling trays and begun producing a few English variations on the style under the name Coolship.

Technicalities

The grist for a lambic beer, by law, must consist of at least 30% wheat, although some brewers add up to 40%. Decoction or temperature-controlled mashing is generally needed to break down the starches in the unmalted wheat. The hop varieties do not really matter, as they are old and largely flavourless, but brewers tend to opt for hops that are less aromatic in the first place, such as Fuggle and Saaz. The wild yeasts that invade the cooling wort cover a wide range of strains, including two varieties of *Brettanomyces*, as well as acid-forming bacteria (acetobacters). They each have their say during the prolonged period of fermentation, as do bacteria that reside in the wooden fermentation cask. The fermentation process works like this. Initially, conversion of some sugars to alcohol takes place alongside the development of some acidity. After a few weeks, wild *Saccharomyces* yeasts take firm control, producing more alcohol, before giving way to *Pediococcus damnosus* bacteria that, over three or four months, create lactic acid. Finally, *Brettanomyces* yeasts set to work, developing a little more alcohol, adding their own spicy, funky flavours and drying out the beer. The character of the lambic is further enhanced by the environment in which it is made. Lambic breweries are often dusty and cobwebby as the brewers fear that sweeping all this away will also remove bacteria vital to the flavour of their beers.

A plain lambic usually offers around 5–6% ABV, while a gueuze hits around 5.5–6.5%. To make kriek (again offering 5–6% alcohol), traditional brewers use whole cherries, which – stones and all – are added to the fermenting lambic. The beer ages on the fruit for several months and the nuttiness of the stones often leads to a distinct almond/marzipan note in the finished beer. To make framboise/frambozen, the raspberries are pulped. In less traditional breweries, fruit juices or extracts may be used.

Some beers are known as oud; the term, meaning old, was originally only applied to lambic that was at least two years old, but now it is widely used for beers that are made in the traditional lambic fashion, as opposed to less authentic copies. Some breweries produce both types.

Read on

Jeff Sparrow, *Wild Brews: Beer Beyond the Influence of Brewer's Yeast* (Brewers Publications, 2005)

Tim Webb, Chris Pollard and Siobhan McGinn, *LambicLand* (Cogan & Mater, 2010)

Visit

There is only one place where a real understanding of lambic can be acquired and that is Payottenland itself. Here, you may find bars serving plain lambic in simple earthenware jugs, just like the local wine in rustic parts of France or Italy. Payottenland is easily accessible by train from Brussels, although the breweries are then spread out over this rural area and not so easy to reach, except by the odd bus and by walking. Happily, there are several lambic-based events organized during the year when the best of the region's products and many of its suppliers are gathered in one place, including the **Weekend of Spontaneous Fermentation** (en.bierpallieters. be), a festival held in the town of Buggenhout in May, when around 70 beers – all authentic, no commercial copycats – can be sampled. Also worth noting is the Dag van de Kriek

(Day of the Kriek), a combination of festival and informative workshop, staged in the town of Eizeringen at the end of May. In even-numbered years, in springtime, there's a further one-night festival, the **Nacht van de Grote Dorst** (Night of the Great Thirst), also hosted by Eizeringen. This festival showcases the best lambic producers and also allows similar beers from around the world to be tasted alongside the originals. In odd years, in April/May, there's the **Toer de Geuze** (Tour of Gueuze) in which a number of breweries throw open their doors to the public for a day. Bus transportation can be booked. Details of all these events can be found at www.dorst.be/evenementen.

For an overview of the lambic scene, **Visitor Center De Lambiek** (www. oudbeersel.com) can be found in the town of Beersel and is open

at weekends from February to Christmas. While there, you can tour the **Oud Beersel brewery** (group visits most of the time by appointment, but individual entrance with no need to book on the first Saturday morning of the month).

If you can't make it out to Payottenland, a great alternative, being very close to the Bruxelles Midi station (the terminus for the Eurostar service), is the **Cantillon brewery** (www.cantillon.be). This is Brussels' last lambic brewery, producing outstanding examples of the genre. It is also a working museum and a tour here is a real eye-opener to the weird and wacky world of spontaneous fermentation. You can round off the visit with a taste of some beer and, if you've never tasted lambic before, it will blow your mind.

TASTE OFF!

Lambics

Cantillon Bruocsella Grand Cru

One of the few plain lambics to be bottled, this is a golden brew with a strong citrus accent and barely a prickle of carbonation. Oranges, lemons and grapefruit feature in a sour, tart taste that leaves an acidic burn at the back of the throat. It's also slightly rustic and musty, with hints of mushroom, and a tannin-like dryness from the oak. An uncompromising introduction to the lambic style.

Oud Beersel Oude Geuze Vieille

Note the huge contrast in carbonation compared with Cantillon Bruocsella: this is a spritzy, golden beer with lots of foam. You can see why some people call gueuze the Champagne of the beer world. Tartness leads the way, but this is a milder tasting beer – delicate, refined and much easier to drink than the plain lambic. Rustic notes feature again before a very dry, lemon-acidic finish.

Boon Oude Kriek

This is a bright claret-coloured beer, with a pink foam. It bursts with lush, jammy cherries and yet doggedly remains tart and acidic, with sweetness kept well in check. Note the almond and marzipan flavours from the cherry stones, and the very dry, faintly bitter finish.

If you want to try more...

... try these other examples:

Plain Lambic: De Cam Oude Lambiek **Gueuze:** Cantillon Gueuze 100% Lambic, De Troch Chapeau Oude Geuze, Hanssens Oude Gueuze **Kriek:** Cantillon Lou Pepe Kriek, Mort Subite Oude Kriek, Oud Beersel Oude Kriek

... you may also like:

Berliner weisse, Flemish red, oud bruin

Wood-aged beers

Beer matured in wooden casks is not a new concept. Take a look at the sections on Old ales and Lambics for evidence of this. However, the idea of allowing beer to age in casks that previously held another liquid is certainly one of the big ideas of the new millennium. Casks that were once used for maturing whisky, brandy, bourbon and other spirits are now in great demand among brewers who are keen to add an upmarket variation to their range.

One of the pioneers of the wood-ageing concept is Innis & Gunn. The story has it that founder Dougal Sharp hit on the idea while working at the Caledonian Brewery in Edinburgh. Caledonian had supplied the William Grant distillery with a quantity of ale that the distillery could use to season former bourbon casks before using them for whisky maturation – the whisky, picking up on the flavours the wood soaked up from the beer, would gain a 'beer finish', in the same way that whisky makers like to create whiskies that have sherry or perhaps port finishes. When the time came for the cask to be emptied and the beer poured away, workers sneaked a quick slurp and liked what they found. Word filtered back to Dougal Sharp who, recognizing the potential of what had been created, set up Innis & Gunn to market the product. Sharp also began experimenting by maturing beer in casks that previously held rum, Scotch whisky and Irish whiskey. Numerous other brewers have joined the party, including fellow Scots Harviestoun, who put a strong version of their Old Engine Oil ale into casks that once held Highland Park whisky to create a beer called Ola Dubh (black oil). Later arrivals included Fuller's, with its Brewer's Reserve selection. The concept is even bigger in the US, where they call it barrel ageing and where former bourbon casks now sell at a premium because of demand among brewers.

Technicalities

Before the arrival of metal casks, nearly all beers would have been stored in, and served from, wooden vessels. The wood – usually oak – worked well in providing a strong, leak-proof container but it had a drawback, namely the influence of the wood itself. Brewers generally did not want the wood to flavour their beers and so they tried to minimize its effect by soaking the casks in boiling water, by acid treatment or by lining the casks with pitch. Today's brewers take a converse approach; what wood can bring to the taste of the maturing beer is usually welcomed. Virgin oak, however, needs to be handled with care, as the raw wood flavours can be overwhelming. Innis & Gunn's Original is matured for 30 days in lightly toasted American white oak barrels that previously held bourbon. This provides powerful vanilla notes that are rounded off by blending the beer with the contents of other casks. Other brewers prefer to use casks that previously contained another drink. Whisky is a popular choice in the UK, because of the availability of casks from Scotland's distilleries. These are mostly former bourbon casks that Scotch whisky makers use a few times before deciding they need to be replaced. Brewers snap these up, hoping their beer will absorb character not just from the wood, but also from the whisky. Some whiskies are matured in former sherry casks, and brewers have also latched onto these. In the US former bourbon casks are conveniently available as, by law, they can only be used once for bourbon.

As casks have become more expensive to acquire, some brewers have looked to alternative methods of achieving similar results. These include ageing beer with oak chips. What such an approach generally fails to provide is a spirit character that, in the case of true barrel ageing, results from spirit flavours that have impregnated the wood seeping into the beer, although Innis & Gunn now uses bourbon-infused oak chips to complement its cask-aged beer.
Inside the cask, over time, the beer also absorbs compounds naturally found in the wood. These range from lipids that bring the typical oaky flavours, vanillin that, as its name suggests, is responsible for vanilla, and tannins that add some astringency.

The actual beer put into the casks for wood maturation varies from brewery to brewery, but the best results come from working with strong ales such as barley wines, IPAs and imperial stouts. Knowing which type of beer to use and how long to allow it to rest in the wood have become new brewing skills, as has the art of blending the beer that emerges with beer from other casks to get the right result.

Visit

For an understanding of how wood influences maturation, a visit to a distillery rather than a brewery is in order. Many distilleries in Scotland welcome visitors, with **Aberlour**, on Speyside, and **Lagavulin**, on Islay, rated among the best and most informative tour experiences. The Discovering Distilleries website (www.discovering-distilleries.com) suggests plenty of opportunities. To sample an extraordinary range of wood-aged beers, you can't beat **Stone Brewing's Oakquinox** (www.stonebrewing.com). It is held at the brewery in Escondido, California, every spring, and, if you're really into wood-ageing, it's worth the trip as more than a hundred different wood-aged beers can be sampled.

TASTE OFF!

Wood-aged beers

Innis & Gunn Original

Note the dominant oak/bourbon flavours, characterized by tangy wood, creamy vanilla and hints of coconut. The base beer contributes a faintly toffee-like malty sweetness and a little kick of warmth.

Harviestoun Ola Dubh Special 21 Reserve

This near-black, bittersweet beer has been aged in oak that matured Highland Park whisky for 21 years. The dark chocolate notes of the roasted grains are well harmonized by the tangy, drying tannins from the oak, hints of coconut and a prominent – but not heavy – whisky presence. Note the spirit-like warmth.

Samuel Smith Yorkshire Stingo

Aged in oak casks that previously held only beer, this is a less-nuanced example. The wood is not new so its impact is modest, but there is still a light oaky tang and a creaminess that enhances that of the malt, as well as a slightly astringent tannin character. Otherwise, a rich red berry and raisin fruitiness holds sway in a mostly sweet, highly quaffable beer for the style and strength (8–9% ABV).

If you want to try more...

... try these other examples:
Franciscan Well Jameson Stout, Fuller's Brewer's Reserve, Innis & Gunn Rum Finish, Old Chimneys Good King Henry Special Reserve, Orkney Dark Island Reserve, Redoak Special Reserve

... you may also like:
barley wine, imperial stout, old ale

Additional styles

In addition to the styles outlined in the previous pages, there are numerous other families of beers that are either not so prevalent or can perhaps be seen as variations on existing styles. These are covered briefly here.

American lager

The speciality of big brewers, the standard American lager is a very pale, delicate, crisp drink, designed for easy quaffing. The common use of adjuncts such as rice and maize reduces the malt impact and the hops employed do not impart strong flavours. A spin-off is the lower-strength lite lager, in which more of the starches are converted to fermentable sugars and fermented away, leaving a leaner beer that is lower in carbohydrates.

Examples: A-B InBev Budweiser, Coors Light, Miller Lite

Black IPA

An oxymoron – purists rage about this style of beer. How can an India pale ale be black? This hasn't deterred brewers, who have sought to marry the coffee and chocolate notes of roasted grains with the piney, fruity notes of expressive hops, creating a kind of cross between a stout and an IPA. An alternative name is Cascadian Dark, which reflects the common use of the Cascade hop in early versions. A lighter-coloured alternative is the red IPA.

Examples: Hardknott Code Black, St Austell Proper Black, Stewart Black IPA

California common

Otherwise known as steam beer (a term now trademarked in the US by Anchor Brewing), this is a type of beer that developed in California during the 19th century, when brewers who had headed west to cash in on the Gold Rush trade tried to produce lagers in a climate that was unsuitable and without refrigeration. The beers consequently fermented at a higher temperature than desired and turned out as a cross between ale and lager that was both crisp and lightly fruity. Release of the high carbonation the beers generated was likened to an escape of steam – one possible derivation of the name.

Examples: Alechemy Stereotype Steam Lager, Anchor Steam Beer, Marston's Revisionist California Common Steam Beer

Champagne beer

Crossing the boundary between beer and wine, some breweries now produce Champagne-style beers. This involves brewing a strong beer and then giving it a secondary fermentation in the bottle, generally using a Champagne yeast. The yeast is then disgorged as in the Champagne process, with the neck of the inverted bottle frozen and the plug of ice at the top that contains the sediment popped out. The result is an elegant beer with a lively, mousse-like effervescence.

Examples: Bosteels DeuS Brut des Flandres, Eisenbahn Lust, Malheur Bière Brut

Green-hop beer

Known as wet-hop beer in the US, this is a type of beer brewed partly, if not entirely, using hops that have just been picked and have not been dried. The result is a more sappy, verdant hop flavour. Because of the need to use the hops quickly, before they deteriorate, the style is most common among breweries based in, or close to, hop-growing areas. Teme Valley Brewery in Worcestershire hosts an annual green-hop beer festival every autumn and there is also a Green Hop Fortnight staged in Kent at the same time of year.

Examples: Gadds' Green Hop Ale, Teme Valley The Hop Nouvelle, Westerham Scotney Green Hop Harvest Ale

Irish red ale

A version of bitter or strong ale, this beer was made traditionally in Ireland with dark malts that imparted a red-brown hue and a prominent malt accent. Largely forgotten for many years, it has been revived in recent decades and is now popular with small breweries, particularly in the US, where it crosses over with American amber ale (see Pale ales & bitters).

Examples: Carlow O'Hara's Irish Red, Killian's Irish Red

Kellerbier

Literally translated as cellar beer, kellerbier is a mostly unpasteurized, mainly Bavarian lager (pale to amber coloured) that is served unfiltered in the biergarten or bar, where earthenware mugs conceal its cloudy appearance. Traditionally, the carbonation was a touch lower than for other lagers, because some of the gas was allowed to escape during maturation. Bottled versions also exist. A similar beer is zwickel, although this is normally just a regular pale lager left unfiltered.

Examples: Hacker-Pschorr Münchner Kellerbier, Köstritzer Kellerbier, St Georgen Keller Bier

Roggenbier

Roggen is the German word for rye, and that tells you much of what you need to know about this type of dark beer from Bavaria. A high proportion of malted rye features in the grist, along with some wheat. The beer is then fermented with an ale or weizen yeast, giving a nutty, sweet, fruity, slightly hazy beer. Other types of rye beer are now being created around the world.

Example: Paulaner Roggen

Scottish ale

Historically, beers in Scotland have had a malt bias, as hops are not commonly grown in the country. This is reflected in the strong style of Scotch ale (discussed in the section on Barley wines) but also in weaker beers, such as 60, 70 and 80 Shilling ales (named after the wholesale price at one time). These are now often grouped under the style banner Scottish ales, although this by no means accurately reflects the diversity to be found in Scottish brewing today.

Examples: Belhaven 80/-, Caledonian Edinburgh Castle, Stewart 80/-

Winter warmer

A seasonal strong ale, usually rich brown in colour and with malt flavours to the fore. It is generally produced as a variation on the modern-day old ale, with some brewers adding seasonal fruits or spices, but the name is particularly associated with the former brewery Young's, whose beer is now brewed by Charles Wells. This started life as a London-brewed version of a style of beer called Burton Ale, which originated in Burton upon Trent but was darker, maltier and sweeter than the town's signature pale ales.

Examples: Samuel Smith Winter Welcome, Young's Winter Warmer

5: The next step

Judging beer

There are hundreds of beer competitions taking place all over the world every year. Some are regional, some are national, some are international. Wherever beer is consumed, it seems that the search is constantly on to find the very best. Becoming part of the judging process is a logical next step for anyone who has taken the trouble to learn and understand about beer. Indeed, judging is a learning process in itself.

Rubbing shoulders with like-minded people, of varying levels of knowledge, is an education, and the basic process of seriously thinking about the beer in front of you, its negative aspects and its merits, working out if it's a better beer than the one before, really does focus the mind. You start to appreciate the technical skills of the brewer as well as the overall appeal of the beer. In a sense, too, being a beer judge formalizes your experience and the knowledge you have acquired. You can even gain qualifications, if you so wish, although by no means do you need diplomas or certificates to start judging.

Judging can be a daunting experience initially, as there are always strong views aired about each beer. It may lead you to question your own knowledge and opinions. Gradually, however, with experience and growing confidence, judges learn to trust their instincts and fight their corner.

Possibly the most accessible beer competitions are those held by CAMRA at its many local events. Most beer festivals aim to select a Beer of the Festival and some act as regional heats for the national Champion Beer of Britain contest. If you are a CAMRA member, you may be able to join one of the judging tables. You'll be seated with fellow CAMRA members or perhaps local brewers and publicans. Sometimes there's a celebrity or a journalist from the local media on the team to drum up a bit of publicity. You'll be briefed about the rules and what criteria are to be used for judging, and there may be some printed guidelines and beer style definitions to follow.

Another way to enter the world of judging is through home-brewers' associations, which organize contests to find the best amateur brewers. Trade competitions, organized by industry magazines or brewing associations, are harder to access as you need to be known to the organizers. Like CAMRA events, they may feature retailers, publicans or journalists, alongside brewers and other experts. The level of knowledge around the tables varies but, with good guidelines to work from, and the presence of technically trained judges in the mix, they manage to combine an element of man-in-the-street experience with specialist knowledge.

One other factor that competition organizers look for in their judges is compatibility with other judges. Although great fun and a wonderful social occasion, beer judging is taken very seriously, and anyone who disrupts the atmosphere is unlikely to be asked to return. Healthy debate is encouraged but a domineering or boorish attitude – no matter how great the judge's knowledge – is not welcomed.

Judging beer is not for all beer lovers; for some, it detracts from the pleasure. But it's certainly true that the judging process can help focus your knowledge and help you get even more out of beer.

Technicalities

Most beer competitions judge beer by style. It is the judges' job to determine which are the best, based not only on their technical merits (no faults or off flavours), quality and character, but also on their adherence to style. It can happen that a technically perfect beer that is agreed to be the best does not win, because it does not strictly conform to the style guidelines being followed. These relate to colour, strength, flavours and other factors that the competition organizers have decided in advance correctly summarize what each style is about. Other competitions are more flexible. They may have looser guidelines or they may not consider style at all.

Judging venues are chosen for their appropriate lighting, temperature and seclusion from distracting noises and smells. Smoking is strictly prohibited and judges are discouraged from wearing perfume/aftershave and eating palate-corrupting foods with strong flavours before the session. Tables are set with individual judging places and furnished with still water, plain crackers or bread, pens, paper, scoresheets, napkins and, sometimes, spittoons.

Beers for judging are presented at the appropriate temperature for the style, in small measures in what is known as a flight. The flight could consist of as few as five or six beers, or as many as 10 or even a few more, commonly arranged in increasing strength order. If a mixture of styles is being considered, darker beers may fall towards the end. Beers are generally presented anonymously, in identical glassware, and identified only by a code number or letter.

As mentioned, each competition has its own rules and guidelines. Most, however, follow the following pattern. As a flight of beer arrives, judges work through each beer individually, without commenting. A judging sheet is provided. This may be broken down into a number of sections, often including space for judges' comments as well as scores. Some forms are designed so that just one beer is evaluated, in detail, per form; others have room for scoring several beers. A typical, very simple form is shown opposite.

You will see that judges are asked to give marks out of a set number for each criterion. Some criteria have a higher weighting of scores because they are seen to be more important. Each judge fills in a score for each beer. After the flight has been completed by all judges there is often a discussion, leading to some judges amending their scores as they consider points made by others. The scores are then tallied and the highest-scoring beers are put through into the next round of judging, where they are compared with the best beers in the same style as judged by another table. The process continues until there is a winning beer, and often runner-up beers. Prizes are then awarded accordingly and the winning beer may progress to a taste-off against the winning beers in other styles to find the best beer in the competition.

One possible drawback of such a judging system is that judges may score wildly differently; some judges may score high and others low. In order to compensate for this, certain tolerances may be introduced, such as all judges on a table needing to score within 10% of each other. This requires some scoring adjustments to be made during the discussion phase. In other competitions, scoring may be abandoned in favour of a simple order of preference, with beers that have most first places or second places, for instance, taking the honours. However, in some of the most prestigious competitions, scoring is not taken into account at all and judges instead discuss and agree which beers are worthy of progression to the next round or worthy of a medal. This can be a lengthy, sometimes heated, process.

Read on

Randy Mosher, *Tasting Beer* (Storey Publishing, 2009)

Gregg Smith, *The Beer Enthusiast's Guide* (Storey Publishing, 1994)

Judging form

	Beer A	Beer B	Beer C	Beer D	Beer E
Appearance /5					
Aroma /10					
Taste /10					
Body/mouthfeel /5					
Aftertaste/finish /10					
Overall impression /10					
Total /50					

Appearance

The process of judging begins with the appearance of a beer. If a beer is being judged according to strict style parameters, the colour is very relevant. A lighter or darker hue than prescribed can lead to disqualification or the removal of a beer to another category. Some judges like to use colour cards, which resemble paint swatches, to confirm the colour of each beer. Clarity is also an issue. Some beers are meant to be hazy and so this is allowed for in the style guidelines, but most beers are not and judges will mark a beer down if there is no good reason for haze. Some judges carry a small torch to check the clarity of darker beers which may be hard to judge in normal light. Then there is the matter of foam. A beer with no head and lacking carbonation is almost always marked down.

Aroma

The next step involves the aroma. Beer is served in small measures, sometimes in special glassware that allows the aroma to be fully appreciated. Judges will often assess the aromas of all of the beers before tasting any of them, fearing flavour contamination. What they are looking for are technical flaws, any hints of production problems. Off flavours, as highlighted earlier, are marked down severely.

Taste

For tasting, judges adopt the same approach outlined earlier in the section on The tasting experience, allowing the beer time in the mouth to tease out all the various flavours, good and bad. Once again, the primary emphasis is on faults but, assuming no faults, judges then compare the flavours they find with the style parameters set down, scoring lower for beers that do not conform precisely. This may involve a mark-down for a beer that has too high a hop profile for the style, or perhaps an unwelcome malt character.

Body/mouthfeel

Another feature to be assessed at this stage is body/mouthfeel. This relates to the thickness and texture of the beer in the mouth and scores are again awarded according to how well the beer conforms to the accepted guidelines for the style.

Aftertaste/finish

Unlike in wine competitions, beer judges swallow. Some like to use spittoons, especially if there are lots of beers to sample, but even these swallow a little of each beer in order to assess the aftertaste or finish. Again, there will be guidelines specifying what flavour components are desired in the finish but judges will also look here for issues such as astringency, cloying maltiness or harsh hop character.

Overall impression

Most judging forms then have a section for overall impression or drinkability. This allows the judge more subjectivity to weigh up the complete package.

Additional information

In some competitions, judges are asked to provide more information than simple scores. There may be sections on the judging form where technical issues can be discussed, possibly even tick-boxes for common faults such as diacetyl, DMS, light-strike and acetaldehyde. This detail is usually required because a copy of the scoring sheet is sent to the brewery with the helpful intention of providing positive feedback on beers that do not win awards.

Visit

There are various training courses and workshops that can be attended to learn how to judge beer. Many American beer judges, if they are not brewers themselves, follow the training provided by the Beer Judge Certification Program (BJCP: www.bjcp. org). This is a structured education in the skills of beer judging, with an examination to pass at the end in order to qualify. The Program is now also holding exams and workshops in other countries. In the UK, the **Beer Academy** (www.beeracademy.co.uk), among other courses, runs a How to Judge Beer one-day course, during which the skills outlined in this chapter are illustrated, focusing on style definitions and boundaries, judging methodologies, identifying off-flavours and the practical evaluation of styles. An exam at the end leads to a certificate.

TASTE OFF!

Judging beer

Take three beers of a given style, say three best bitters. Below are given the CAMRA and BJCP guidelines for this style (see Visit on p189) – note how they differ in some respects and in the level of detail. Work through the judging process as outlined above, using the information about tasting beer provided earlier in this book, and see how you would rank the beers accordingly, after identifying any technical problems or style anomalies. To repeat the exercise with other beers, you can find CAMRA's beer style guidelines online at www.camra.org.uk/different-styles and the BJCP's guidelines at www.bjcp.org.

CAMRA guidelines

Best bitters are more robust than ordinary bitters. They are typically brown, tawny, copper, or amber but can be paler. They have medium to strong bitterness, light to medium body but with a more evident residual maltiness. A strong hop character should be evident and diacetyl (toffee/butterscotch) should be minimized. Fruit should be limited, although citrus fruit tastes are associated with some hop varieties.

Original gravity: 1040 up to less than 1046

Typical alcohol by volume: 4.0–4.6%

Bitterness: 20–40 EBU*

* European Bitterness Units

CAMPAIGN
FOR
REAL ALE

BJCP guidelines (© Beer Judge Certification Program, Inc.)

11B. Best Bitter

Overall impression: A flavorful, yet refreshing, session beer. Some examples can be more malt balanced, but this should not override the overall bitter impression. Drinkability is a critical component of the style.

Aroma: Low to moderate malt aroma, often (but not always) with a low to medium-low caramel quality. Bready, biscuit, or lightly toasty malt complexity is common. Mild to moderate fruitiness. Hop aroma can range from moderate to none, typically with a floral, earthy, resiny, and/or fruity character. Generally no diacetyl, although very low levels are allowed.

Appearance: Pale amber to medium copper color. Good to brilliant clarity. Low to moderate white to off-white head. May have very little head due to low carbonation.

Flavor: Medium to moderately high bitterness. Moderately low to moderately high fruity esters. Moderate to low hop flavor, typically with an earthy, resiny, fruity, and/or floral character. Low to medium maltiness with a dry finish. The malt profile is typically bready, biscuit, or lightly toasty. Low to moderate caramel or toffee flavors are optional. Balance is often decidedly bitter, although the bitterness should not completely overpower the malt flavor, esters and hop flavor. Generally no diacetyl, although very low levels are allowed.

Mouthfeel: Medium-light to medium body. Low carbonation, although bottled examples can have moderate carbonation.

Comments: More evident malt flavor than in an ordinary bitter; this is a stronger, session-strength ale.

History: See comments in category introduction.

Characteristic ingredients: Pale ale, amber, and/or crystal malts. May use a touch of dark malt for color adjustment. May use sugar adjuncts, corn or wheat. English finishing hops are most traditional, but any hops are fair game; if American hops are used, a light touch is required. Characterful British yeast.

Style comparison: More alcohol than an ordinary bitter, and often using higher-quality ingredients. Less alcohol than a strong bitter. More caramel or base malt character and color than a British Golden Ale. Emphasis is on the bittering hop addition as opposed to the aggressive middle and late hopping seen in American ales.

Vital statistics:

IBUs: 25–40

SRM: 8–16

OG: 1.040–1.048

FG: 1.008–1.012

ABV: 3.8–4.6%

Commercial examples: Adnams SSB, Coniston Bluebird Bitter, Fuller's London Pride, Harvey's Sussex Best Bitter, Shepherd Neame Master Brew Kentish Ale, Timothy Taylor Landlord, Young's Special

* Abbreviations stand for:

OG: Original Gravity

IBU: International Bitterness Units

FG: Final Gravity

SRM: Standard Reference Method (This refers to a BJCP colour chart; the higher the number the darker the beer.)

ABV: Alcohol by Volume

Becoming part of the *beer-judging process* is a logical next step

Insight

Some important global beer competitions are listed below.

Champion Beer of Britain: After regional qualifying rounds, this contest takes place on the first day of CAMRA's Great British Beer Festival every summer. The focus is only on cask-conditioned beers from the UK (with one category for bottle-conditioned beers). Beers are awarded medals by style, with a taste-off between all the winners to decide the year's Champion Beer.

SIBA National Beer Competition: Divided into awards for cask, keg and bottle/can, the Society of Independent Brewers' major contest is judged at its annual beer festival and exhibition, Beer X, every spring. Like CAMRA's awards, beers qualify via a number of regional heats held at SIBA or CAMRA beer festivals.

World Beer Cup: Held every other year in a different city in the US, to coincide with the Craft Brewers' Conference, the World Beer Cup attracts entries from all over the globe, although the vast majority of beers judged are American. The number of categories grows every year and now extends to around 100. It is judged in the same way as the competition for American beers held at the Great American Beer Festival in Denver every autumn, with the selection of judges rigorously controlled.

International Beer Challenge: An offshoot of the British trade magazine Off Licence News, this is an annual event held in London but receiving entries from more than 30 countries. Judges are a mix of brewers, retailers, supermarket buyers, beer writers and flavour analysts.

World Beer Awards: This international competition is judged by trade experts in three centres – in Japan (Asian and Oceanic entries), in the US (entries from the Americas) and in the UK (European entries). The winning beers from each group come together for a second round of judging in the UK, with the final round in London opened up to a larger group of judges from within the industry.

Brussels Beer Challenge: Staged in a different Belgian city every November, this is another international event, attracting some of the most knowledgeable judges from around the world.

International Brewing Awards: Formerly known as the Brewing Industry International Awards, and founded in 1886, this competition is judged every two years in Britain and welcomes entries from around the world. Categories include cask, keg and small pack beers (bottles and cans). All judges are professional brewers.

Beer & food

The increasing perception of beer as a connoisseur's drink has been helped, undoubtedly, through the new interest in pairing beer with food. Championed at an early stage by writer Michael Jackson and given added support by the likes of Susan Nowak, Lucy Saunders and Garrett Oliver, the idea of matching beers to gourmet dishes has attracted the attention of many of the world's top chefs, some of whom have gone on to introduce beer menus to sit alongside their wine lists in their Michelin-starred restaurants.

The fact that such illustrious names as Michel Roux, Raymond Blanc and Jamie Oliver have all taken time to understand the concept, reveals that beer really does have a place in gourmet circles. That said, some of the world's best beer pairings come with the simplest of meals. Sausage and mash illustrates the message just as well as paté de foie gras.

So what is it that beer brings to the dining table? Clearly one of its greatest assets is its versatility. Wine, of course, is the first drink most people consider when dining out but let's just look at the flavours wine can offer. Essentially, it boils down to degrees of sweetness and dryness, various types of fruitiness or herbiness, perhaps some nutty or floral notes, a level of acidity, and some oak influence if the wine has been aged in wood. This is a gross simplification, I concede, and is in no way intended to disparage what is one of the world's greatest drinks. But think about the flavours beer can offer. In this book, we look closely at beers that are pale, bright and spritzy, perhaps laced with zesty citrus notes. We also consider beers that are quite the opposite – dark, moody and rich, wallowing in flavours of chocolate and coffee. In between, there are beers that feature flavours as varied as raisins, vanilla, cherry, liquorice, toffee, ginger, nut and assorted tropical fruits, from banana to pineapple. Then there are speciality creations such as smoked beers and wood-aged beers. And we're not talking mere suggestions of such flavours, as might be teased out by a wine buff: these are big flavours, integral to the make-up of these beers.

This clearly puts beer in a much better position than wine for flavour matching, as does the fact that beer is usually carbonated, whereas most wines are not. The carbonation is useful in that it cleanses the palate between mouthfuls of food, the bubbles stripping away fat and creaminess. This is a particular asset when cheese is on the table.

The other great advantage beer has over wine is in price. Because beers – even the best beers in the world – are so much cheaper than wines, it is possible to have a different beer for each course of a dinner, rather than having to choose a wine that will have to cope with whatever has been selected for starter and main course, and possibly also cheese and dessert.

There are still many people sceptical about the idea of beer and food pairing but, if the above points are not enough to sway them, then perhaps there is one further thought they should bear in mind. Beer and food is a traditional partnership. Beer is what people in many countries naturally consumed with their meals for many centuries, long before the increasing influence of the wine industry saw the beer bottle booted off the table. As we know, there are many lessons to be learned from history. I would suggest beer and food pairing is one.

Some of the world's *best beer pairings* come with the simplest of meals

Tip

If you plan on serving beer with a multi-course meal, don't allow too much beer for each dish. A pint with each course may appeal to some but it will quickly fill you up. A good wine glass makes an appropriate measure and helps avoid bloating.

Technicalities

It may be argued that any beer does the job with food. Certainly, I never object if a glass of beer is offered, whatever I'm eating but, to really understand the pairing concept, and to take your appreciation of beer to another level, there are certain basic principles you need to follow.

In order for the beer to enhance the food, rather than detract from it – and indeed for the food to enhance the beer – you first need to consider the intensity. By this I mean how full-bodied and full-flavoured a beer is. The level of alcohol also comes into this. There is no point in pairing a delicate poached fish dish with a big, boisterous barley wine, for example, as all the subtleties of flavours in the food will be blown away. Far better to select something pale and elegant, perhaps a clean pilsner or a Belgian witbier.

The next step is to consider the flavours of the beer and which flavours in the food they will go well with. Here there are two approaches that can be taken. The first is to complement the flavours in the food, matching like with like. The idea is to find linking or harmonizing flavours on each side. Some people call this

A *crisp, sharp and spritzy beer* will counteract any oiliness in the food

a bridge. So, if you have a chargrilled burger, a porter with the same caramelized, toasted notes links well. Or, if you're serving a salad with a vinaigrette dressing, a Flemish red or oud bruin, with its own acidic notes, can do the business.

The alternative approach is to find a contrast, choosing a beer that has flavours quite different from those found in the food. Logically this should not work, but very often it does. It's something we do every day, even without beer in the picture. Think of the classic combinations of peanut butter and jam, turkey and cranberry, cheese and chutney. Consequently, you might consider a German weizen, with its apple and spice notes, alongside roasted pork. Or you might well find that a chocolate pudding explodes into life when enjoyed with a Belgian kriek. Sometimes, though, things don't work out. Get the wrong pairing and you can really end up with a clash of flavours. But, when you get things right, it can be sensational.

Whichever approach you consider, complementary or contrasting, keep foremost in your mind how bitter the beer is. This is one aspect of beer's complexion that can let it down with food and gives wine an advantage point. Bitterness can be a huge asset – in counteracting salty food, for instance – but it can also jar horribly in the wrong circumstances, especially with desserts. You wouldn't want to drink a hoppy pilsner with a sweet pudding.

The final factor to consider is the character of the food and the texture of the beer. It may be that you need something crisp, sharp and spritzy to keep any oiliness or creaminess under control. A lightly acidic, well-carbonated beer is just the right counterpoint to oily fish, for example. In other circumstances, something velvety and malty-thick, with low carbonation, will work better, as in the case of spicy foods (such as a hot curry) where the richness of the beer tempers the spices and gives respite from the heat.

Tip

Sometimes, for a great beer and food pairing, you just need to take a leaf out of our ancestors' book and pick up on some combinations traditionally experienced around the world. There's a reason why Bavarians drink weizen with pork knuckles, why the Belgians quaff witbier with mussels, and why Britons once commonly downed stout with oysters.

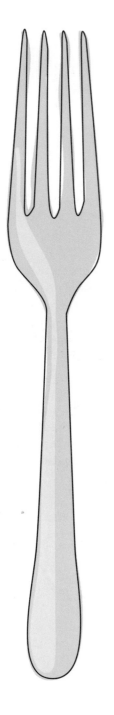

Elementary beer pairing ideas

Here are some basic suggestions for beers to accompany various dishes.

Before dining

Aperitif	Bitter; kriek; pilsner; witbier

Starters

Fish	Golden ale; helles; pilsner; witbier
Pasta	Cream-based sauce – golden ale; weizen
	Pesto – pilsner; tripel
	Tomato-based sauce – amber ale; Vienna
Pâté	Dubbel; dunkel; mild
Quiche/soufflé	Weizen
Risotto	Tripel; weizen
Shellfish	Stout; witbier
Soups	Vegetable – golden ale
	Meaty – brown ale

Main courses

Barbecue	Brown ale; dunkel; porter; smoked beer
Beef	Bitter; brown ale; dubbel
Chicken	Vienna; weizen
Curry	Bock; weizen
Duck	Bière de garde; dubbel; Flemish red; witbier
Gammon	Helles; pilsner; smoked beer
Goose	Dubbel
Lamb	Bière de garde; brown ale; dunkel
Liver	Dubbel
Lobster	American pale ale; kölsch
Meat pie	Brown ale; dubbel; strong ale
Mexican	American pale ale; chocolate beer; dunkelweizen; Vienna
Oriental	Ginger/spiced beer; weizen; witbier
Pheasant	Brown ale; dubbel; Flemish red
Pizza	Amber ale; Vienna lager

Ploughman's	Bitter; strong ale
Pork	Dunkel; pilsner; weizen
Sausages	Bitter; dunkel; strong ale
Turkey	Brown ale; dubbel
Venison	Dubbel; witbier

Vegetables

Asparagus	Tripel
Avocado	American pale ale
Lentils	Brown ale; dunkel
Mushrooms	Brown ale; dunkel
Nuts	Brown ale; dunkel
Peas	Weizen
Salad	Flemish red; weizen; witbier
Spinach	Weizen
Sweetcorn	Helles; weizen

Cheese

Goat's	Kriek; weizen
Mature/blue	Barley wine; dubbel; IPA; old ale
Mild	Golden ale; weizen
Strong	Barley wine; dubbel; IPA; strong ale

Desserts

Apple/banana	Weizen
Cheesecake	Imperial stout; kriek; porter; sweet stout
Chocolate/coffee	Kriek; porter; stout
Creamy	Barley wine; stout
Fruitcake	Barley wine; weizenbock
Fruit tart	Kriek; stout
Ice cream	Barley wine; imperial stout; kriek; porter; sweet stout
Red berry	Kriek; porter
Spiced	Weizen

TASTE OFF!

The following pages illustrate some experiments I've attempted to get an understanding of how beer and food pairing works. Focus has been placed on staple dishes and popular ethnic alternatives but the same principles apply to more extravagant culinary creations. Try these out for yourself, perhaps adding your own beer input.

Fish & chips

A number of beers have been created specifically to pair with fish. Sharp's Chalky's Bite, developed with TV chef Rick Stein and featuring the delicate herbal notes of wild Cornish fennel, is one, and it does work very well with certain seafoods. However, the traditional British fish and chip takeaway presents a more robust challenge. It calls for a beer that can rip through the oiliness of the food and, I think, offer a little complementary flavour – ideally a citrus note to emulate a squeeze of fresh lemon on the batter. So a solid British bitter would seem to be the answer here. I chose Coniston Bluebird Bitter. It's a crisp, fresh, peppery ale with lots of citrus character but one that is also delicate enough not to overpower the food. It was a good choice, with the added bonus of a brisk carbonation to cut through the fat. Maltier ales, such as Banks's Mild, can also work well, with the malt notes echoing the same in the malt vinegar that is often sprinkled on top.

Next I opened a weizen, knowing that the Bavarian wheat beer style, with its low bitterness, high carbonation and complex fruit and spice flavours, is an excellent choice for a wide variety of dishes. It didn't work out this time. The beer I chose, the very good Hefe Weissbier Hell from Weltenberger, had just too much banana flavour to work with the fish. On the other hand, its creamy sweetness married supremely well with the mushy peas I had warmed up as a side.
The real star of the show was a witbier, Hitachino Nest White Ale, from Japan. The lemon-citrus sharpness proved just perfect at slicing through the greasiness of the batter and contrasting with the earthy flesh of the flaky fish. With lots of bubbles from the heightened natural carbonation, it also cleansed and refreshed the palate.

Beef stew

There are many types of beef stew, with ingredients varying from country to country. Some, of course, include beer in the gravy (such as in the classic Belgian carbonnade), in which case an ideal match (if unadventurous) would be the same beer as in the pot. For other stews, basically you'd be looking for something rich and malty as a beer accompaniment, as I found when pairing beers with a simple casserole of organic beef with pearl barley and lots of sweet root vegetables. I went for brown ales of varying types. The first option, Manns Brown Ale, had just the right degree of sweetness and dark grain character but, being only 2.8% ABV, lacked the body and depth to really hold its own. The second beer, Anchor Brekle's Brown, was substantial enough for the job and offered a caramel note that blended in rather well with the food but, as is typical of the US brown ale style, it was simply too fruity and hoppy. The best combination came via the strong, dark Belgian ale Gouden Carolus Classic, brewed by Het Anker brewery. For a strong beer, it is rather slight in body, and in this respect it was a touch lightweight, but the sweetness was a perfect match for the sweetness of the carrots and parsnips, and the caramel malt flavours married wonderfully with the darkness of the meat.

Shellfish

Logic would suggest that delicate items such as seafood – unless heavily flavoured by a sauce – would require a delicate beer, but there's also a received wisdom that stout is an ideal match. This derives from the fact that Londoners commonly drank stout or porter with oysters in Victorian times. I put the idea to the test by preparing three simple seafood plates. First up, not risking an oyster, I served some pre-cooked cockles. I resisted the temptation to souse them in vinegar and tasted them plain. I found them quite gritty and salty and the first beer I opened really didn't offer anything to improve them. This was Blanche de Namur, a witbier from Belgium. It's by no means a bitter beer but it just didn't deliver enough sweetness, and its lemon-like, peppery coriander notes failed to enhance the cockles. I also tried the fuller, sweeter, creamier Innis & Gunn Original, an oak-aged beer with rich vanilla, mild toffee and interesting coconut notes. Its creaminess nicely wrapped up the cockles and the sweetness countered the salt. It was a nice combination but the beer smothered the fish a little. The third option was Hook Norton Double Stout, a beer that has a firm bitter roasted character, as well as some chocolate and coffee notes. I didn't expect

A *pint* and a *ploughman's* is one of the simplest food pairings

much but was amazed at how well the food and the drink went together. The roasted dryness of the beer washed away the salt and the chocolate notes added sweetness. It really worked.

The same three beers then went head to head with some simply prepared crab (a mix of white and dark meat). Crab is sweet and salty, with its own light creaminess. The witbier paired well, the spicy fruitiness adding a nice contrast and its natural sweetness on a par with that of the crab. The oak-aged beer also tied up the sweetness well and the vanilla and coconut notes seemed to slot in seamlessly but, as with the cockles, it was just a bit too dominant. After the first test, I had high hopes for the stout but it didn't work at all. It was a real clash of flavours.

Finally, I lightly seasoned and quickly fried some fresh scallops. Scallops are sweet but very delicate and the witbier unfortunately overpowered them. The oak-aged beer was, again, perhaps a touch too sweet and rich, but its complex flavours did marry well. If I had caramelized the scallops a little more, I think the vanilla and gentle toffee flavours would have worked even better. As for the stout, the bitterness and dryness did add a nice contrast but there was just a touch too much chocolate for a good pairing.

The lesson I learned is that shellfish, in all its glorious variety, needs to be treated on a case-by-case basis, and that it takes a little trial and error to achieve the perfect match. But the potential is certainly there for some stunning combinations.

Chinese dishes

I resisted the temptation to select a strongly spiced beer to go with Chinese food. I considered a ginger beer and also Hop Back's lemongrass-infused Taiphoon, but opted just for three regular beers. A weizen (Erdinger Weissbier) and a witbier (Wadworth Beer Kitchen Wheat Beer) were chosen for their delicate spice notes and crisp, well-carbonated character; a dubbel (Westmalle) was added for its darker flavours and vinous qualities. On the food side, I chose a fairly typical combination of Chinese dishes, starting with vegetable spring rolls and spare ribs, and moving on to beef in black bean sauce, chicken chow mein and sweet and sour chicken. There is a wide spectrum of flavours in that combination and I knew the beers were going to be seriously tested. I doubted I would find one beer that could cover all bases and was proved right.

Because of their earthy flavour, anything with beansprouts involved, such as the spring rolls, needs a sweeter beer. The witbier was just the ticket, especially as the carbonation cut through the slight oiliness of the rolls. The dubbel also fared

well, its delicate fruit notes accentuated by the vegetables. Dubbel was also a good pairing with spare ribs, rubbing along nicely with the sweet, charred notes of the pork, although the weizen was even better. The delicate apple flavours of the beer complemented the meat perfectly and the raised carbonation really zipped through the fat.

Chicken chow mein was a difficult proposition. I struggled to find anything that really provided a wow factor, although the weizen came closest, proving again that this is really a very competent food beer. As for the sweet and sour, well, this was always going to be a test, and the witbier failed it, the sweetness of the beer jarring against the sugary notes in the food. The dubbel, with its winey character, held its own but the best combination was with the weizen, that dealt comfortably, if not spectacularly, with both the sugar and the vinegar in the sauce.

Indian dishes

I'm always confused at the sight of people ordering wine in an Indian restaurant. Beer, surely, is a better option. But what do you need for a successful beer and curry partnership? Well, it begins with sufficient strength to handle the burn of chilli and continues with good carbonation and plenty of body to cleanse and soothe the palate. It's tempting to think just of strong ale or lager but, looking for something a bit different in the hope of teasing out something special, I picked up some less obvious beers – a strong stout, a fruit beer and a barley wine. I then raided the local takeaway and came up with a handful of typical dishes, kicking off with some onion bhajees and pairing them with Lion Stout from Sri Lanka. It didn't seem likely that a chunky sweet, chocolatey stout would fit at all well, but the richness of the beer calmed the fire in the spices while the sweeter notes tied in beautifully with the caramelized sweetness of the onions. I next dug into some prawn bhuna, a rather salty, fishy curry that really came to life with Charles Wells Banana Bread Beer. This is not a beer I particularly care for as a drink on its own, but with certain foods that dominant banana flavour can work a treat and it really did here, providing a stunningly exotic contrast.

I then tried to match the earthy lentil flavours of a vegetable dhansak with the earthy hops and fruit of Chiltern's Bodgers Barley Wine, and with some success, and the same beer also coped nicely with the exotic warmth of chicken madras and the spinach bitterness of sag aloo. But it was Banana Bread that again scored best when it came to the dhansak, and also to tangy chicken rogan, really refreshing the palate.

IPA is, for many people, the ideal accompaniment, but I've found it can only work well as long as the hop character is not too strident. There are, as I discovered, more rewarding combinations.

Mexican dishes

There is a wide variety of flavours in a Mexican meal. It's not just about chilli and beans. I prepared a combination of dishes to cover all bases and picked on a trio of diverse beers to see what really gelled. I felt the mixture of beans, beef, avocado, rice, tomatoes and chilli across the dishes called for something a little richer than a pilsner, a pale ale or a weizen, so I opted for Brooklyn Lager, which, at heart, is a Vienna – one of Mexico's brewing specialities – but also has the citrus qualities of a US pale ale, suggesting to me a good counterpoint to the peppery citrus note of coriander in a salsa. While a plain weizen always fares well at the table, by choosing a dunkelweizen (Weihenstephaner Hefeweissbier Dunkel) I gave myself some roasted grain character to play with, and I then threw in a maverick, a chocolate beer (Hogs Back Montezuma's Chocolate Lager). Mexicans like a spot of chocolate mole on their plates so I thought this would add the same variety.

There were some stunning combinations. Guacamole with the chocolate beer was remarkable, with the sweetness and creaminess of the chocolate blending beautifully with the avocado. The same beer also paired well with refried beans, comparing favourably with the dunkelweizen that also was a good match for spicy Mexican rice. The best complement to steak chilli was Brooklyn Lager, as the caramel notes in the beer enriched the beefiness of the dish, but this was where the chocolate beer didn't quite hit the spot. Finally, I prepared some fajitas, stuffing corn wraps with salsa, spiced onions and peppers, which the dunkelweizen dealt with admirably, matching the sweetness of the vegetables and calming down the spices without preventing the flavour of the food shining through. Overall, the best all-rounder was the dunkelweizen but it seems chocolate beer can create some amazing partnerships.

Spaghetti al pesto

With its bold, distinctive flavours, pesto presents an interesting challenge for beer pairing. The sauce is basically a combination of garlic, olive oil, pine nuts, basil and Parmesan cheese. It's slightly salty, fairly rich and full of herbal flavours. The ideal beer would seem to be one that has plenty of body to match the fullness of flavour, good carbonation to cut through the cheese and oil, and a hoppy/spicy character to provide a counterpoint to the tangy notes of pine nut, garlic and herbs. Although the dish is Italian (and there are no doubt some excellent Italian beers that are man enough for the job), I felt something Belgian, with its raised alcohol, spicy complexion and balanced hoppiness would make a good fit. I kicked off with a pale ale. De Ranke XX Bitter is golden in colour and noted for its bold hop character. It turned out to be too bold. The herbal notes were just about right but the bitterness was too strong. Next I opened a Chimay Tripel, knowing that this would be less assertively bitter. It was a far better match, with the raised carbonation and bittersweet taste tying in very nicely. There's also a slight orange fruitiness, however, and that clashed just a little. The best option proved to be Duvel, the classic strong Belgian blond. This ridiculously quaffable, 8.5% ABV beer had just the right level of crispness and fizz, with hints of lemon in the hops that didn't clash with the pesto. I don't think I found the perfect companion in the three beers I tried but I don't think I was too far off either.

Cheese

It is often thought that wine is the obvious partner to cheese but beer can work far better, as many wine experts will secretly admit. This is not just because beer has that lively carbonation that can cleanse the palate and cut through the fat that cheese leaves on the tongue, but also because beer and cheese have certain synergies. You can make a case that beer and cheese are traditional partners. Both are natural agricultural products – indeed both originating as grasses – often

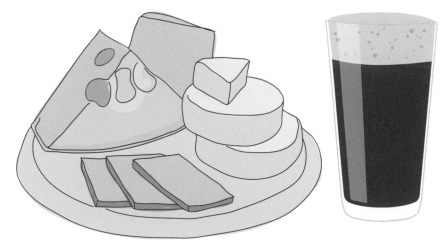

produced together on farms in times past and consumed together in a break from ploughing fields or herding cows. These days they are both seen as high-quality, artisan products. But more important is the variety of flavours on both sides. It can be hard to find a wine that doesn't swamp a delicate cheese or has the guts to stand up to a mature cheese. With beer, you can take your pick.

To put this to the test, I sampled a trio of cheeses: a French Brie, milky and gentle with an earthy rind and a mushroom-like finish; an extra mature Cheddar, creamy but tangy and biting, with crunchy salt crystals; and a Stilton, creamy but salty, with earthy blue veining. The three beers I set them against were Maredsous Blond, a fairly sweet, medium-bodied, fruity beer from Belgium with a notably dry finish; Hook Norton Flagship, a robust English-style IPA; and Fuller's Vintage Ale 2007, aged for more than seven years so that hop character had declined and fortified wine oxidation notes had developed.

The best combination with the Brie proved to be the Maredsous, which was delicate enough not to drown out the cheese. The light acidity of the beer seared through the fat and the fruit added a tropical contrast, yet the earthiness of the cheese rind was still able to shine through. Both the Flagship and the Vintage Ale worked well but were simply too bold for this cheese, the former swamping it with hops and the latter overwhelming it with its lush notes of butter toffee and dried vine fruits.

The Maredsous also dovetailed nicely with the Cheddar, although it seemed a little underpowered for the strength of the cheese. The Flagship worked better, with the tanginess of the hops facing off the tanginess of the cheese, although the hops eventually ran out the winner and some of the appeal of the cheese was diminished as a result. The weight of the Vintage Ale was just perfect, however, helping develop a thick, bittersweet taste combination, enhanced by the grape-like contrast of the beer's fruit notes.

Finally, the complexity and boldness of the Stilton were just too much for the Maredsous. The flavour matching was fine, but the character of the beer was blown away, leaving just cheese and bitterness. Once again the hops in the Flagship proved a touch too dominant for the cheese – although it was by no means a poor partnership – leaving the best combination to come with the Vintage Ale. This beer really freshened the palate, absorbed the spiky sharpness of the cheese and wrapped it all up in a rich, bittersweet smoothness, with fruit again a nice counterpoint.

Overall, there may have been winners in this experiment, but there were no losers. Cheese and beer are indeed natural partners. To achieve perfection, you just need to ensure the right balance of weight and flavour intensity.

Visit

If you have some cash to splash, it will be of interest to pay a visit to a pub or restaurant that specializes in beer and food pairing. Here are some European options (there are many more in the US, where beer pairing in brewpubs is commonplace).

Anchor, Walberswick, Suffolk (www.anchorat walberswick.com)

De Groote Witte Arend, Antwerp, Belgium (www.degrootewittearend.be)

Den Dyver, Bruges, Belgium (www.dyver.be)

Hotel Restaurant Erasmus, Bruges, Belgium (www.brasserieerasmus.com)

Lowlander Grand Café, Covent Garden, London (www.lowlander.com)

Old Brewery, Greenwich, London (www.oldbrewery greenwich.com)

Restobières, Brussels, Belgium (www.restobieres.eu)

White Horse, Parsons Green, London (www.whitehorsesw6.com)

Chocolate pudding

Sweetness in a dessert can be a real test for beer, and the pudding I tried – a dark sponge with a sticky chocolate sauce – was really quite sweet. Up against it were three contrasting beers. I started with Moncada's Notting Hill Porter, which has quite a strong roasted-grain flavour for the style. Porters are generally a touch sweeter than stouts and the bitterness of this particular beer was a touch too heavy, even though its chocolate and coffee flavours were ideal. Next I tried Zywiec Porter, a potent example of the Baltic porter style of lager. My bottle had been ageing for a few years and so had lost some its early hoppy snappiness and mellowed into a creamy, sweet raisin fest that proved a far better companion for the pudding than the weaker, younger porter. Finally, as a contrast, I poured out some Boon Kriek. This is a really lush kriek, loaded with juicy cherries and hints of marzipan. It is sweeter than more authentic kriek lambics but by no means as sickly as some of the most commercial; the background tartness and acidity ensure that. I loved it with the pudding. The acidity cut through the sweetness of the sauce and the richness of the sponge, and the fleshy cherry flavours brightened everything up, creating a Black Forest gateau sensation in the mouth.

Fruit cake

A simple Genoa cake, well filled with raisins and sprinkled with a few cherries; that was the test for three beers that I selected primarily for their sweetness. First up was Andechs Bergbock Hell, a golden heller bock from Germany, one that is loaded with body-building, sweet, sugary malt. That aspect of the beer was ideal but the brewers have also balanced that malt with a generous dosing of hops. That's great for simple drinking but not so good for this pairing exercise, as the herbal bitterness they added really didn't synch in. Much better was Sambrook's No. 5, a barley wine with its own fruit-cake character. With the cake it was a dream, the texture and fullness were perfect and the sweet, buttery malt and raisin notes a seamless continuation of the flavours in the cake. Its strength also helped, adding a boozy dimension that really lifted a piece of humble cake into a luscious dessert. Finally, I was convinced that a big, powerful weizenbock, with all those fruity, spicy weizen flavours ramped up to the full, would really hit the spot with a cake like this. I chose Schneider Aventinus and was not disappointed. The banana, apple, clove and marzipan complexity of the beer sparked nicely off the fruit in the cake and the body and sweetness were, once again, spot on.

Visit

Look for special dinners organized by beer writers or other experts and any food-and-beer sampling sessions that may be laid on by breweries. Alternatively, the **Beer Academy** (www.beeracademy.co.uk) hosts regular beer-and-food-matching courses in various UK venues. For those with a professional interest in the subject, it also runs sessions to test and accredit beer sommeliers.

Insight

When carefully thought through and well executed, a full-on beer and food pairing dinner is one of life's great pleasures. Here are a couple of examples of successful dinners.

Menu for the
*British Guild of Beer Writers'
Annual Dinner*
at the Carlton Jumeirah hotel in Knightsbridge, London, on
5 December 2013.

✳

Lemongrass- and Chilli-marinated Salmon with Cornish Crab and Guacamole

Camden Hells Lager, 4.6%

✳

Pot Roast Norfolk Pheasant, Venison Sausage Roll, Caramelized Brussels Sprouts and Chestnuts, Smoked Garlic Mash

Wild Beer Modus Operandi, 7%

✳

Manjari Chocolate Moelleux, Dulcey Chocolate Centre, Salted Caramel and Stout Ice Cream

Partizan Quad, 11.2%

✳

Petits Fours

Williams Bros Alba, 7.5%

Dinner hosted by
Goose Island brewery
at the White Horse,
Parsons Green, London, on
12 September 2008. All beers were brewed by Goose Island.

✳

Mini Yorkshire Puddings with Rare Roast Beef and Hot Horseradish

Goose Island IPA, 5.9%

✳

Mussel Bree
Fresh English mussels in white wine and cream soup

Matilda, 7%

✳

312 Urban Wheat Sorbet

✳

Roast Stuffed Goose & Seasonal Vegetables (a four-bird roast with duck, partridge and pigeon)

Honkers Ale, 4.3%

✳

Chocolate & Vanilla Torte with Vanilla Ice Cream

Bourbon County Stout, 11%

✳

Award-Winning British Cheeses

Keen's Cheddar, Colston Bassett Blue Stilton, Stinking Bishop

Pere Jacques, 9%

Cooking with beer

'If there's liquid in a recipe, it might as well be beer', claims Australian actor and chef Paul Mercurio. That's true up to a point for, while beer may make a brilliant accompaniment to food, it is more problematic when used in the food itself. The major issue is bitterness: most beers are simply too hoppy to build into a recipe, and if you reduce the beer by boiling it down, the bitterness only increases. You also have to be careful with malty beers, as the sugars can caramelize in the saucepan. Of course, there are times when you may want either effect, a biting hop character or a caramel note, but these are the things that often catch out would-be beer chefs. Quantities are also a very difficult area; generally, a little beer goes a long way.

More experienced practitioners, of course, have it all down to a fine art. There are some seriously brilliant beer chefs around the world, some building on traditions in countries such as Belgium and Germany, others heading off on flights of fantasy, latching on to the creations of today's adventurous brewers to bring a new dimension to the dining table.

If you fancy a crack at beer cuisine, here are some ideas of how beer can be used. Detailed recipes can be found in the cookbooks mentioned below.

Read on

Stephen Beaumont, *The Beer & Food Companion* (Jaqui Small, 2015)

Fiona Beckett and Will Beckett, *An Appetite for Ale* (CAMRA Books, 2007)

Mark Dredge, *Beer and Food* (Dog 'n' Bone, 2014)

Janet Fletcher, *Cheese & Beer* (Andrews McMeel, 2013)

Richard Fox, *The Food and Beer Cook Book* (Senate Books, 2006)

Paul Mercurio, *Cooking with Beer* (Murdoch Books, 2011)

Susan Nowak, *The Beer Cookbook* (Faber and Faber, 1999)

Garrett Oliver, *The Brewmaster's Table* (HarperCollins, 2003)

Lucy Saunders, *The Best of American Beer and Food* (Brewers Publications, 2007)

Schuyler Schultz, *Beer, Food and Flavor* (Skyhorse Publishing, 2012)

Ben Vinken, *Belgian Beer on the Menu* (Editions Lanoo, 2010)

Uses for beer in cooking

Beer	How to use in cooking
Blond abbey beer	Freshening up a cheese fondue
Brown ale	As part of the topping for Welsh rarebit
Citrus-accented pale ale Kreik/framboise	Reduced into a sorbet
Dunkel	To enrich the sauce for braised pork
Flemish red Framboise	As the basis for a vinaigrette
Kriek/framboise	To add zip to a fruit pudding
Pale ale	As part of a marinade for barbecued ribs
Pale ale Witbier	To lighten a beer batter, for frying or making pancakes
Stout Porter	To deepen the flavours of a chocolate truffle or mousse
Strong ale	In the gravy of a steak and ale pie
Trappist ale	Adding character to a thick meaty stew (carbonnade)
Witbier	As the liquor for cooking mussels

Over to you!

Thank you for reading this book. I'm conscious that it has packed in a lot of information, some of which has been rather advanced. I hope, however, that if you've reached this page you will now feel far more confident about your beer knowledge than when you started reading.

The pages have now run out. I can't fit in any more and it's really over to you. By following up the Visit and Read on suggestions in the book, you can take your knowledge to new levels. Wider reading, of course, helps too. Specialist magazines such as *All About Beer* (allaboutbeer.com) from the US and *Beer & Brewer* (www.beerandbrewer.com) from Australia feature entertaining reports and reviews by leading writers and, if you join CAMRA (www.camra.org.uk), you will receive the award-winning *Beer* magazine four times a year free of charge. Also, think about following some of the many beer bloggers on the internet. The level of expertise varies, of course, and you may not agree with any opinions expressed, but it will help you keep up to speed with happenings in the world of beer and to consider new ways of thinking about a particular topic. My own online magazine, *Inside Beer* (www.insidebeer.com), also has topical features, news, reviews and event information.

Undoubtedly, though, the best way to further your knowledge is to keep sampling beers. But do so methodically. As outlined earlier in the book, making and keeping tasting notes is an important way of understanding beer. It makes you think about what you are drinking and is a convenient way of comparing beers over a period of time. Reading about each beer, its history and style as you taste adds depth to your understanding, and comparing findings with trusted experts via books or the internet makes the experience even more absorbing. I've been writing professionally about beer for more than 25 years and, by making notes, reading and comparing, I'm always learning something new.

Where you take your newly-acquired beer expert status is up to you. You can use it for your own personal satisfaction or you can impress your friends. You may want to become more involved by becoming a judge or an accredited beer sommelier. Perhaps it will help you embark on a career in the industry or launch your own blog. Information is power. Use it wisely!

Where you take your newly-acquired *beer expert* status is up to you

Jargon busting

A quick guide to the technical terms that can often bamboozle the beer drinker. (See also the tables earlier on flavours and off-flavours.)

ABV: Alcohol by Volume – the percentage of alcohol in a beer (the strength).

Adjuncts: other cereals and sugars which are added to malted barley during brewing, often to create a cheaper beer but sometimes for special flavours or effects.

Aftertaste/afterpalate: see Finish.

Ale: a top-fermenting beer (the yeast mostly sits on top during fermentation).

Alpha acid: the principal bittering agent found in hops.

Aroma: the perfumes given off by a beer.

Attenuation: the replacement of sugars by alcohol through the action of yeast during fermentation. An over-attenuated beer is thin and dry; an under-attenuated beer is sweet and full-bodied.

Autolysis: the breakdown of yeast in aged beer, giving rise to savoury flavours.

Body: the fullness of the beer, generally related to malt content.

Bottle-conditioned: beer that undergoes a secondary fermentation in the bottle (real ale in a bottle).

Bottom fermentation: the yeast falls to the bottom during fermentation (typical of lager yeasts).

Brewery-conditioned: beer with a fermentation completed at the brewery and usually pasteurized.

Bright: beer that has been drawn off its yeast or filtered to be clear.

Burtonize: to adjust the salts in brewing water to emulate the natural, hard waters of Burton upon Trent.

Carbon dioxide: a gas naturally created by yeast during fermentation and vital to the drinkability of a beer; see also Condition.

Cask: container for unfiltered, unpasteurized beer.

Cask-conditioned: beer given a secondary fermentation in a cask (real ale).

Chill proofing: removing solids from beer that would cause haze at low temperatures.

Cold break: cooling of wort to remove proteins and other material.

Condition: the amount of dissolved carbon dioxide in a beer. Too much and the beer is gassy; too little and it is flat.

Craft beer: a problematic, loose term often used to describe beer from small(ish), new(ish), independent breweries that is commonly packaged unpasteurized in kegs (but can also be in casks). In the US, the term is more specifically defined and takes into account the size and ownership of the business and the primary ingredients used (malt rather than cheap adjuncts).

Decoction: a continental mashing system in which parts of the wort are moved into a second vessel and subjected to a higher temperature, before being returned to the original vessel. The aim is better starch conversion into sugar.

Dry hopping: the process of adding hops to a beer after it has been brewed, usually in the cask or in a conditioning tank prior to bottling, in order to enhance the hop character and aroma.

Esters: organic compounds consisting of an alcohol and an acid, produced during fermentation, that often add fruity or floral aromas and flavours.

Ethanol: alcohol created by fermentation; also known as ethyl alcohol.

Extract: the amount of sugar in the wort.

Fermentation: the conversion by yeast of sugars into alcohol and carbon dioxide.

Filtered: a beer with its yeast and other sediment extracted; sterile-filtered beer has passed through a very fine filter.

Final Gravity (FG): see Original Gravity.

Finings: a glutinous liquid that attracts yeast particles and draws them to the bottom of a cask, leaving the beer clear. Finings are usually made from the swim-bladder of a tropical fish. Also known as isinglass.

Finish: the lingering taste in the mouth after swallowing beer.

Flocculation: the natural clumping together of yeast cells.

Green beer: beer that is not fully matured.

Green hops: hops picked fresh from the bine and used without undergoing the traditional drying process that allows them to be stored for months. Green hops provide a pungent, sappy character.

Grist: crushed malt ready for mashing. The term also refers to a mix of cereals, or hops, used in the brew.

Gyle: a batch of beer.

Hot break: the boiling of wort to remove proteins and other material.

Infusion: a mashing process involving soaking grains in hot water.

Isinglass: see Finings.

Isomerization: the conversion of hop components during the boil to enhance the bitterness and increase solubility.

Keg: a pressurized container for storing beer – usually a beer that has been pasteurized. Brewery-conditioned beers, or keg beers, need gas pressure to give them artificial fizz.

Kräusen: to add a small quantity of partially-fermented wort to a beer in order to provide fresh sugars for the yeast to continue fermentation. It helps generate extra condition.

Lager: a bottom-fermented beer (the yeast sinks to the bottom of the wort during fermentation) that is matured for several weeks (months in the best instances) at low temperatures.

Late hopping: the process of adding hops late to the copper boil, to compensate for any aroma that may have been lost from hops used earlier in the boil.

Lightstrike: the effect on beer of exposure to bright light. This can cause a chemical reaction, leading to unsavoury aromas and flavours. Also known as sunstrike.

Liquor: the name used in breweries for brewing water.

Malt extract: commercially produced concentrated wort, used by some brewers to save mashing, or to supplement their own wort.

Mash: the infusion of malt and water in the mash tun, which extracts fermentable materials from the grain.

Milling: crushing the grains prior to mashing.

Mouthfeel: the texture and body of a beer.

Nose: see Aroma.

Original Gravity (OG): a reading taken before fermentation to gauge the amount of fermentable material in a beer. The higher the OG, the more fermentables and the greater the likely strength of the finished brew. Final Gravity, or FG, is a reading of the density of the wort after fermentation.

Oxidation: the deterioration in beer caused by oxygen, usually manifested in a wet paper or cardboard taste.

Palate: the sense of taste.

Parti-gyle: method of brewing more than one beer at the same time, using one standard brew but adding water to change the strength, or using the first runnings from the mash tun to make a heavy beer and later runnings for a lighter beer.

Pasteurized: beer which has been heat-treated to kill off remaining yeast cells and prevent further fermentation.

pH: the level of acidity in water or in a mash; the higher the number the greater the acidity.

Pitching: adding yeast to a brew to start fermentation.

Priming: the process of adding extra fermentable sugars to a beer to enable a secondary fermentation in the cask or bottle.

Rack: to run beer from a tank or a cask.

Real ale: an unpasteurized, unfiltered beer which continues to ferment in the vessel from which it is dispensed (cask conditioned or bottle conditioned).

Saccharification: the conversion of starches in malt into sugars.

Sediment: solids in beer, primarily yeast but also possibly some proteins.

Single-varietal: a beer using just one variety of hops or one type of malt.

Sparging: spraying mashed grains with hot water to gain more extract.

Sterile-filtered: see Filtered.

Sunstrike: see Lightstrike.

Temperature-controlled mashing: the adjustment of the temperature during mashing to facilitate starch extraction and conversion.

Top fermentation: the yeast mostly sits at the top during fermentation (typical of ale yeasts).

Trub: proteins, yeast and other solid matter extracted during brewing.

Ullage: waste beer; also the space allowed above beer in a container.

Wort: the unfermented sweet liquid produced by mashing malt and water.

Index

Books for beer lovers

CAMRA Books, the publishing arm of the Campaign for Real Ale, is the leading publisher of books on beer and pubs. Key titles include:

Good Beer Guide 2016

Editor: Roger Protz

CAMRA's *Good Beer Guide* is fully revised and updated each year and features pubs across the United Kingdom that serve the best real ale. Now in its 43rd edition, this pub guide is completely independent with listings based entirely on nomination and evaluation by CAMRA members. This means you can be sure that every one of the 4,500 pubs deserves their place, plus they all come recommended by people who know a thing or two about good beer.

£15.99 ISBN 978-1-85249-327-1

Good Bottled Beer Guide

Jeff Evans

A pocket-sized guide for discerning drinkers looking to buy bottled real ales and enjoy a fresh glass of their favourite beers at home. The new eighth edition of the *Good Bottled Beer Guide* is completely revised, updated and redesigned to showcase the very best bottled British real ales now being produced, and detail where they can be bought. Everything you need to know about bottled beers; tasting notes, ingredients, brewery details, and a glossary to help the reader understand more about them.

£12.99 ISBN 978-1-85249-309-7

The CAMRA Guide to London's Best Beer, Pubs & Bars

Des de Moor

The essential guide to London beer, *London's Best Beer, Pubs & Bars* is packed with detailed maps and easy-to-use listings to help you find the best places to enjoy perfect pints in the capital. Laid out by area, the book will be your companion in exploring the best pubs serving the best British and world beers. The venue listings are fully illustrated with colour photographs and include a variety of real ale pubs, bars and other outlets, with detailed information to make planning any excursion quick and easy.

£12.99 ISBN 978-1-85249-323-36

Britain's Beer Revolution

Roger Protz & Adrian Tierney-Jones

UK brewing has seen unprecedented growth in the last decade. Breweries of all shapes and sizes are flourishing. Established brewers applying generations of tradition in new ways rub shoulders at the bar with new micro-brewers. Headed by real ale, a 'craft' beer revolution is sweeping the country. In *Britain's Beer Revolution* Roger Protz and Adrian Tierney-Jones look behind the beer labels and shine a spotlight on what makes British beer so good.

£14.99 ISBN 978 1 85249 321 9

Cellarmanship

Real ale is leading the beer revolution in Britain and outperforming almost every other drink on the bar. With increased numbers of brewers making it, pubs selling it and people trying it, there's never been a better time to master how to keep, store and serve cask ale. *Cellarmanship* is a must-have book if you are a professional or student in the drinks trade, a beer festival organiser or you just want to serve a decent pint at a private event.

£8.99 978-1-85249-331-8

Brew Your Own British Real Ale

Graham Wheeler

The perennial favourite of home-brewers, *Brew Your Own British Real Ale* is a CAMRA classic. This new edition is enhanced and illustrated. Written by homebrewing authority Graham Wheeler, *Brew Your Own British Real Ale* includes detailed brewing instructions for both novice and more advanced home-brewers, as well as comprehensive recipes for recreating some of Britain's best-loved beers at home.

£14.99 ISBN 978-1-85249-319-6

The Beer Select-O-Pedia

Michael Larson

The Beer Select-O-Pedia is a an enthusiast's guide through the delicious world of beer, demystifying scores of traditional and innovative new styles from Britain & Ireland, Continental Europe and America. Organised in families of beer styles according to their origins, it is easy to look up the style of beer you are drinking and discover more. Much more than a list of recommended brews and breweries, this book gives beer lovers all the information they need to navigate the ever expanding world of beer and find new brews to excite their tastebuds.

£12.99 ISBN 978-1-85249-318-9

Great British Pubs

Adrian Tierney-Jones

Great British Pubs is a practical guide that takes you around the very best public houses in Britain and celebrates the pub as a national institution. Every kind of pub is represented in these pages with categorised listings featuring full-colour photography illustrating a host of excellent pubs from the seaside to the city and from the historic to the ultra-modern. Articles on beer brewing, cider making, classic pub food recipes and traditional pub games are included to help the reader fully understand what makes a pub 'great'.

£14.99 ISBN 987-1-85249-265-6

Order these and other CAMRA books online at **www.camra.org.uk/books**, ask at your local bookstore, or contact: CAMRA, 230 Hatfield Road, St Albans, AL1 4LW. **Telephone 01727 867201**

A campaign of two halves

Campaigning for Pub Goers & Beer Drinkers

CAMRA, the Campaign for Real Ale, is the not-for-profit independent voice of real ale drinkers and pub goers. CAMRA's vision is to have quality real ale and thriving pubs in every community. We campaign tirelessly to achieve this goal, as well as lobbying government to champion drinkers' rights. As a CAMRA member you will have the opportunity to campaign to save pubs under threat of closure, for pubs to be free to serve a range of real ales at fair prices and for a long term freeze in beer duty that will help Britain's brewing industry survive.

Enjoying Real Ale & Pubs

CAMRA has over 175,000 members from all ages and backgrounds, brought together by a common belief in the issues that CAMRA deals with and their love of good quality British beer. From just £24 a year* — that's less than a pint a month — you can join CAMRA and enjoy the following benefits:

* Subscription to *What's Brewing*, our monthly colour newspaper, and *Beer*, our quarterly magazine, informing you about beer and pub news and detailing events and beer festivals around the country.

* Free or reduced entry to over 160 national, regional and local beer festivals.

* Money off many of our publications including the *Good Beer Guide*, the *Good Bottled Beer Guide* and CAMRA's *So You Want to be a Beer Expert*.

* Access to a members-only section of our national website, www.camra.org.uk, which gives up-to-the-minute news stories and includes a special offer section with regular features.

* Special discounts with numerous partner organisations and money off real ale in your participating local pubs as part of our Pubs Discount Scheme.

Log onto www.camra.org.uk/join for CAMRA membership information.

*£24 membership cost stated is only available via Direct Debit, other concessionary rates available. Please note membership rates stated are correct at the time of printing but are subject to change. Full details of all membership rates can be found here: www.camra.org.uk/membershiprates